DEVELOPING LANGUAGE
Writing 1

Starting Points for Writing

Peter Dougill
English Adviser, West Sussex County Council

Sue Hackman
Teacher of English, Queen Mary's College, Basingstoke

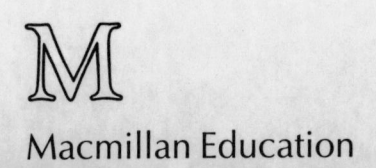

Macmillan Education

© Peter Dougill and Sue Hackman 1987

All rights reserved. No reproduction, copy or transmission of this publication may be made without written permission.

No paragraph of this publication may be reproduced, copied or transmitted save with written permission or in accordance with the provisions of the Copyright Act 1956 (as amended), or under the terms of any licence permitting limited copying issued by the Copyright Licensing Agency, 7 Ridgmount Street, London WC1E 7AE.

Any person who does any unauthorised act in relation to this publication may be liable to criminal prosecution and civil claims for damages.

First published 1987

Published by
MACMILLAN EDUCATION LTD
Houndmills, Basingstoke, Hampshire RG21 2XS
and London
Companies and representatives
throughout the world

Designed by Linda Reed

Printed in Hong Kong

British Library Cataloguing in Publication Data
Dougill, Peter
Starting points for writing. —— (Developing language skills. Writing; 1).
1. English language —— Composition and exercises
I. Title   II. Hackman, Sue   III. Series
808'.042   PE1408
ISBN 0-333-43938-4

Contents

Preface   v

1   Writing for yourself   1

    Keeping a diary   1
    Letters   8
    Spelling   14
    Finding inspiration   18
    Improving work   24
    Presenting work   30

2   Picture this   41

    Picture words   41
    Education AD 3000   42
    The deserted house   45
    Cartoon strips   46
    Picture book   54

3   Writing to get things done   55

    Holiday brochure   55
    Theme park   59
    Promoting music   60
    Words only   60
    Telling how   64

4   Telling tales   68

    Oral literature   68
    Mini-sagas   69
    Cautionary tales   76
    Pocket stories   78
    Twisted tales   82
    Extracts   84

5	**Journeys in your mind**	**90**
	Travelogues	90
	Mission Improbable	97
	Mounting an expedition	99
	Imaginary island	100
	Town trail	101
6	**Publications**	**103**
	Book covers	103
	Class magazine	106
	Poetry anthology	108
	Commissioning a novel	110

Preface

The suggestions for writing that this book provides have all been tried and tested in the classroom, and have grown out of work with a cross-section of pupils in comprehensive schools. Essentially, they have all proved themselves as enjoyable tasks, which have helped the students concerned to progress as independent writers.

The two Writing books in this series were then compiled with GCSE firmly in mind. They aim to fulfil the National Criteria's demands for content as applied to the 'writing' domain:

> Opportunities must be provided to develop a variety of styles of writing in what may be termed 'closed' situations (e.g. the writing of letters, reports and instructions) where the subject matter, form, audience and purpose are largely 'given', and in what may be termed 'open' situations (e.g. narrative writing and imaginative/personal response to a range of stimuli and experience) where such factors are largely determined by the writer. Response to reading may include the opportunity to write factually or imaginatively in developing and exploring themes and ideas arising from what is read.

The whole range of assignments therefore provides a variety of 'closed' and 'open' contexts as well as a combination of short and extended pieces of work.

We believe most firmly that writing is not just about the finished product, the piece of work that's handed in to the teacher, but also about the process, the things that go on in your mind while you are composing your work. We believe that the writing process is a thinking process. We hope that some of the strategies and opportunities suggested here will help you to become a better writer, not just in your English lessons but also in other subjects, and in your outside life as well.

1 Writing for yourself

Make a list of all the occasions on which you have written over the past week: telephone messages? homework? shopping lists? Then consider these questions:
- How much writing do you do?
- Who reads it?
- Why do you do it?
- When and where do you prefer to write?
- What strengths and weaknesses do you notice in your own writing?
- Which aspects of your work do you most need to improve?

A great deal of the writing you do is for other people, often teachers, and you do it because you are told to! But writing is a powerful way of thinking through ideas for yourself. It is a way of learning, planning and expressing what you think.

In this section, we offer a number of ideas to make writing more helpful and interesting.

Keeping a diary

Keeping a diary will:
- [ ] put your experiences into perspective
- [ ] help you to find a comfortable style
- [ ] encourage fluency

Perhaps you already keep a diary. Many famous writers find a diary essential for their work. Regular entries will keep your ideas flowing and help you to express yourself easily and naturally. Also, it is often said that keeping a diary is a way of getting to know yourself better.

Here is an extract from a diary which is almost 200 years old:

from: The Diary of a Farmer's Wife, 1796–7

Aug. ye 20. – This be the first time I hav writ in my book for three dayes, bein bussie.

It hav bin a verrie hot day and we to church at night, after the milking be don and the pigges fed.

The passon was new, and did preche a verrie prosie surmon, so I nearly aslepe, and did jump much at the last himm singeing. I was glad to be out once more, and John bidden the passon to supp with us we back home, where Sarah cumming in, we did put the supper reddie in the best kitchen.

Aug. ye 21. – Up yester morn att 4 off the clocke, and carters wiffe cumming we to the washing; getting all reddie for the hangeing out before breakefuste.

John in to saye Dollie the red cow be sicke, so me to make a drink for her good, it bein chill. I do warme sum milk, to which I do put a spoon full of breesed appel pips and 2 egges, all shook upp with a glass of brandie, which John do give her. Later she much better, and John did give her milk to the calfs.

Carters wiffe do say Emma Tranter hav got an arm broke through falling from off their tallet steppes; and that Farmer Joneses Marye be getting wed to Bill Somers, at which I be not surprised, hearing a whisper anon. But I doute me if they hav got much to start on, the old Jones be farelie warm, so folkes do say.

TWO SHEEP LOST

Later John cum in to say Farmer Ellis be cum, lookeing for 2 sheep which he hav lost, and much fears they be stol. Wher on carters wiffe do up and say she did see two strange men in the village yester eve; which be verrie odd to my thinkinge, as I do say to Farmer Ellis when I out to the gate with a tot of cyder for him. And he agrees, so he be off to the squire to see about it; and I back to the kitchen feeling verrie sorrie for the poor wretches if they hav done the stealing, for it be a serious thing to steal a shepe.

Aug. ye 23. – Me and Sarah bein bussie with lime washen of the kitchen and house place, John hav to feed the pigges and calfs, which do fuss him much; and the big boar pigg biting him hard on the leg, he cums in most wrotheful, and sayes he will hav us out cum tomorrow. At which I do say how can we when we so bussie? So he off out agen after hitting the cat with my pewter pepper pot.

Then in cums Sarah with her hand all bloddie, and she crieing, saying she did do it with the big carver. This I do wash and tye with a peece of old shirt.

John in agen do say whats ado, and me telling him, he mighty cross, saying it be all done apurpus to vex him and not to go out to help him. Indeed he be verrie wrothe.

JOHN OVERHEARS ...

At this I be so cross I uppes and sayes Sarah be my maid not his, and he to get out of my kitchen till his temper be better. So he out, shutting the door with a grate noise, saying that wimmen was the verrie divvell; at which I so wrothe I did throw a lump of bredd at him, but only hit the shut doore. Then I did pictur to myself Johns face if I had hit him, and fell to laffing so hartilie that the tears did run adown my cheekes. John do think he be such a grett man, but lord he be just a bigge sillie.

Then me telling Sarah all, she do say: make him a pan cake, and he soone better.

ANNE HUGHES

For the next week, try keeping a detailed diary about the everyday events in your life. It may be useful to bear the following points in mind:
- You don't need a formal diary to write in. An old exercise book will do and you can put in your own headings.
- You don't have to have an eventful life to write a worthwhile diary. Life is made up of small events, feelings and details which are important in their own way.
- You may have more to write on some days than on others. Take each day separately, but always try to write *something* – regularity does help. Put aside half an hour. Don't be put off if you run dry: few ideas are instant.

Writing for yourself

- There are no rules about what to include in your diary. Any events, ideas or thoughts which interest you are worth writing about.

Fictional diaries

Fictional diaries are entertaining to read and to write. Here are extracts from two fictional diaries:

from: The Secret Diary of Adrian Mole, aged 13¾

Wednesday   May 6th

I am proud to report that I have been made a school-dinner monitor. My duties are to stand at the side of the pig bin and make sure that my fellow pupils scrape their plates properly.

Thursday   May 7th

Bert Baxter rang the school to ask me to call round urgently. Mr Scruton told me off, he said the school telephone was not for the convenience of the pupils. Bert was in a terrible state. He had lost his false teeth. He has had them since 1946, they have got sentimental value for him because they used to belong to his father. I looked everywhere for them, but couldn't find them.

I went to the shops and bought him a tin of soup and a butterscotch Instant Whip. It was all he could manage at the moment. I have promised to go round tomorrow and look again. Sabre was happy for once; he was chewing something in his kennel.

My father is still cleaning the house up. Even Nigel commented on how clean the kitchen floor looked.

Friday   May 8th

Found Bert's teeth in Sabre's kennel. Bert rinsed them under the tap and put them back in his mouth! This is the most revolting thing I have ever seen.

My father has got bunches of flowers to welcome my mother home. They are all over the house stinking the place out.

Mr Lucas's house has been sold at last. I saw the estate agent's minion putting the board up. I hope the new people are respectable. I am reading the *Mill on the Floss*, by a bloke called George Eliot.

Saturday   May 9th

I was woken up at 8.30 by a loud banging on the front door. It was an Electricity Board official. I was amazed to hear that he had come to turn off our electricity! My father owes £95.79p. I told the official that we needed electricity for life's essentials like the television and stereo, but he said that people like us are sapping the country's strength. He went to the meter cupboard, did something with tools, and the second hand on the kitchen clock stopped. It was dead symbolic.

SUE TOWNSEND

from: *Flowers for Algernon*

progris riport 1 – martch 5 1965

Dr. Strauss says I shud rite down what I think and evrey thing that happins to me from now on. I dont know why but he says its importint so they will see if they will use me. I hope they use me. Miss Kinnian says maybe they can make me smart. I want to be smart. My name is Charlie Gordon. I am 37 years old and 2 weeks ago was my brithday. I have nuthing more to rite now so I will close for today.

progris riport 2 – martch 6

I had a test today. I think I faled it. and I think that maybe now they wont use me. What happind is a nice young man was in the room and he had some white cards with ink spilled all over them. He sed Charlie what do you see on this card. I was very skared even tho I had my rabits foot in my pockit because when I was a kid I always faled tests in school and I spilled ink to.

I told him I saw a inkblot. He said yes and it made me feel good. I thot that was all but when I got up to go he stopped me. He said now sit down Charlie we are not thru yet. Then I dont remember so good but he wantid me to say what was in the ink. I dint see nuthing in the ink but he said there was picturs there other pepul saw some picturs. I coudnt see any picturs. I reely tryed to see. I held the card close up and then far away. Then I said if I had my glases I coud see better I usally only ware my glases in the movies or TV but I said they are in the closit in the hall. I got them. Then I said let me see that card agen I bet Ill find it now.

I tryed hard but I still coudnt find the picturs I only saw the ink. I told him maybe I need new glases. He rote somthing down on a paper and I got skared of faling the test. I told him it was a very nice inkblot with littel points all around the eges. He looked very sad so that wasnt it. I said please let me try agen. Ill get it in a few minits becaus Im not so fast somtimes. Im a slow reeder too in Miss Kinnians class for slow adults but I'm trying very hard.

He gave me a chance with another card that had 2 kinds of ink spilled on it red and blue.

He was very nice and talked slow like Miss Kinnian does and he explaned it to me that it was a *raw shok*. He said pepul see things in the ink. I said show me where. He said think. I told him I think a inkblot but that wasnt rite eather. He said what does it remind you – pretend something. I closd my eyes for a long time to pretend. I told him I pretned a fowntan pen with ink leeking all over a table cloth. Then he got up and went out.

I dont think I passd the *raw shok* test.

progris report 3 – martch 7

Dr Strauss and Dr Nemur say it dont matter about the inkblots. I told them I dint spill the ink on the cards and I coudn't see anything in the ink. They said that maybe they will still use me. I said Miss Kinnian never gave me tests like that one only spellin and reading. They said Miss Kinnian told that I was her bestist pupil in the adult nite scool becaus I tryed the hardist and I reely wantid to lern. They said how come you went to the adult nite scool all by yourself Charlie. How did you find it. I said I askd pepul and sumbody told me where I shud go to lern to read and spell good. They said why did you want to. I told them becaus all my life I wantid to be smart and not dumb. But its very hard to be smart. They said you know it will probly be tempirery. I said yes. Miss Kinnian told me. I dont care if it herts.

Later I had more crazy tests today. The nice lady who gave it me told me the name and I asked her how do you spellit so I can rite it in my progris riport. THEMATIC APPERCEPTION TEST. I dont know the frist 2 words but I know what *test* means. You got to pass it or you get bad marks. This test lookd easy becaus I coud see the picturs. Only this time she dint want me to tell her the picturs. That mixd me up. I said the man yesterday said I shoud tell him what I saw in the ink she said that dont make no difrence. She said make up storys about the pepul in the picturs.

I told her how can you tell storys about pepul you never met. I said why shud I make up lies. I never tell lies any more becaus I always get caut.

She told me this test and the other one the raw-shok was for getting personalty. I laffed so hard. I said how can you get that thing from inkblots and fotos. She got sore and put her picturs away. I dont care. It was sily. I gess I faled that test too.

Later some men in white coats took me to a difernt part of the hospitil and gave me a game to play. It was like a race with a white mouse. They called the mouse Algernon. Algernon was in a box with a lot of twists and turns like all kinds of walls and they gave me a pencil and a paper with lines and lots of boxes. On one side it said START and on the other end it said FINISH. They said it was *amazed* and that Algernon and me had the same *amazed* to do. I dint see how we could have the same *amazed* if Algernon had a box and I had a paper but I dint say nothing. Anyway there wasnt time because the race started.

One of the men had a watch he was trying to hide so I wouldnt see it so I tryed not to look and that made me nervus.

Anyway that test made me feel worser than all the others because they did it over 10 times with difernt *amazeds* and Algernon won every time. I dint know that mice were so smart. Maybe thats because Algernon is a white mouse. Maybe white mice are smarter then other mice.

Writing for yourself

> *progris riport 4 – Mar 8*
>
> Their going to use me! Im so exited I can hardly write.
>
> DANIEL KEYES

Now you try writing a fictional diary, or continue one of the extracts.

Letters

Letter-writing will help you:
- ☐ to master an important and popular form of communication
- ☐ to express your personality, thoughts and feelings on paper
- ☐ to trust words when you cannot see or hear your reader

In a group, discuss these questions.
- What sorts of letters have you written in the past?
- What sorts of letters do you receive? What are your reactions to them?
- What sorts of letters do you expect to write later on in life which you do not write now?
- When is a letter more appropriate than a telephone call or a visit?
- Which letters are the most difficult to write? Why?

Now read the following letters. (The sequence on pages 9–11 was written during the Second World War.) Discuss your reactions to them.

No. 2001/Cambs/7393
(If replying, please quote above No.)

Army Form B. 104—83

[Stamp: RECORD OFFICE WARWICK 3 APR 1942]

......................................Record Office,

....19 .

~~Sir or~~ Madam,

I regret to have to inform you that a report has been received from the War Office to the effect that (No.) 5933485 (Rank) Pte (Name) WHITE Robert Frank (Regiment) THE CAMB'S REGT was posted as "missing" on the 15 FEB 1942 at Singapore.

The report that he is missing does not necessarily mean that he has been killed, as he may be a prisoner of war or temporarily separated from his regiment.

Official reports that men are prisoners of war take some time to reach this country, and if he has been captured by the enemy it is probable that unofficial news will reach you first. In that case I am to ask you to forward any postcard or letter received at once to this Office, and it will be returned to you as soon as possible.

Should any further official information be received it will be at once communicated to you.

I am,

~~Sir or~~ Madam,

Your obedient Servant,

R.H.Phillips Capt for Colonel

Officer in charge of Records.

IMPORTANT.
Any change of your address should be immediately notified to this Office.

Wt. 30051/1249 400,000 (16) 9/39 KJL/8812 Gp 698/3 Forms/B.104—83/9

Writing for yourself

俘虜郵便 泰俘虜收容所 濟関検

SERVICE DES PRISONNIERS DE GUERRE

Name R.F. WHITE
Nationality BRITISH
Rank PRIVATE
Camp No: 4 P.O.W. Camp, Thailand.

To:-
MRS. R.F. WHITE
16 POPLAR TERRACE,
STAPLEFORD, CAMBS.
ENGLAND.

IMPERIAL JAPANESE ARMY

Date JUNE 2. 44

Your mails (~~and~~ ——————) are received with thanks.
My health is (good, ~~usual, poor~~).
~~I am ill in hospital.~~
I am working for pay (~~I am paid monthly salary~~).
~~I am not working.~~
My best regards to MAY, MUM, DAD, BETTY AND FAMILY

Yours ever,

Bob

Letters

Telephone: MAYFAIR 9400.

Your Ref. _____

W.O. Ref. SS/330/120/2814.
(Cas.P.W.)

THE WAR OFFICE,
CURZON STREET HOUSE,
CURZON STREET,
LONDON, W.1.

20.9.45.

Madam,

I am directed to inform you with pleasure that official information has been received that your husband. 5933485. Pte. R. F. WHITE. SUFFOLK REGIMENT. previously a prisoner of war in Japanese hands, has been recovered and is now with the Allied Forces.

The repatriation of recovered prisoners of war is being given highest priority, but it will be appreciated that some time must elapse before they reach the United Kingdom. Information of a general character regarding these recovered prisoners, including their movements before they reach home, will be given from time to time on the wireless and will be published in the press.

I am, Madam,
Your obedient Servant,

Mrs. M. White
16 Poplar Terr
Stapleford
Cambs.

Writing for yourself

GRADGRIND MANUFACTURING CO.

Grub Street Mill
Grub Street
Smogtown
Smogshire

Date: As postmark

Dear <u>A. Jones</u>,

Thank you for your application for the post of <u>Assistant Grinder</u>. We regret that we are unable on this occasion to offer you a position in the company. May we take this opportunity of wishing you every success in your career.

Yours sincerely

Miss. P. Lennox

pp. G. Smuggerton
<u>Asst. Personnel Manager</u>

A letter of rejection

> 29 Boston Road
> Bradville
> Yorkshire
> YK16 3ND
>
> 19 February 1987

Dear Jill,

    I do apologise, but I won't be able to come to your birthday party next week. Thank you for inviting me, but my friend Sally has decided to have a party that day, and I don't want to disappoint her. Theresa will also be going to Sally's party and she told me to tell you that she can't come to your party, either. See you next term.

        Love,
          Sharon.

A letter declining an invitation

Some letters are awkward to write. It can be useful to practise writing a difficult letter before you settle on the final wording.

In a group, discuss the problems involved in writing each of the following:
- a letter of sympathy
- a letter of complaint
- a letter of apology
- a letter asking for attention, a favour or friendship
- a letter that will disappoint the reader
- a letter on which a great deal depends

Choose two or three of these awkward letters. Think of situations to which they might apply. Try wording each letter. Then discuss your ideas and any problems you had in writing them.

Spelling

This section will help you:
- ☐ to correct spellings
- ☐ to remember tricky spellings
- ☐ to make the best use of the help available

Most of us worry about spelling. What is the best way to learn a spelling?

Try again yourself

Before you reach for the dictionary, try the difficult spelling again for yourself. Ask someone who is good at spelling whether you have got it right. If you have – good! If you haven't, ask for a *clue*, such as:
   'There's a letter missing.'
   'The letters are in the wrong order.'
   'There are two letters too many.'
In this way you will learn to correct your own spellings.

Keep a record

It is useful to keep a spelling book of these second tries.

Spelling

Ask a parent, friend or teacher to test you on these words to see whether the correct spellings have sunk in. If they have, cross the words off your list. If you still get the spellings wrong, leave them on.

This, for example, is a page from the spelling book of a student called Amanda:

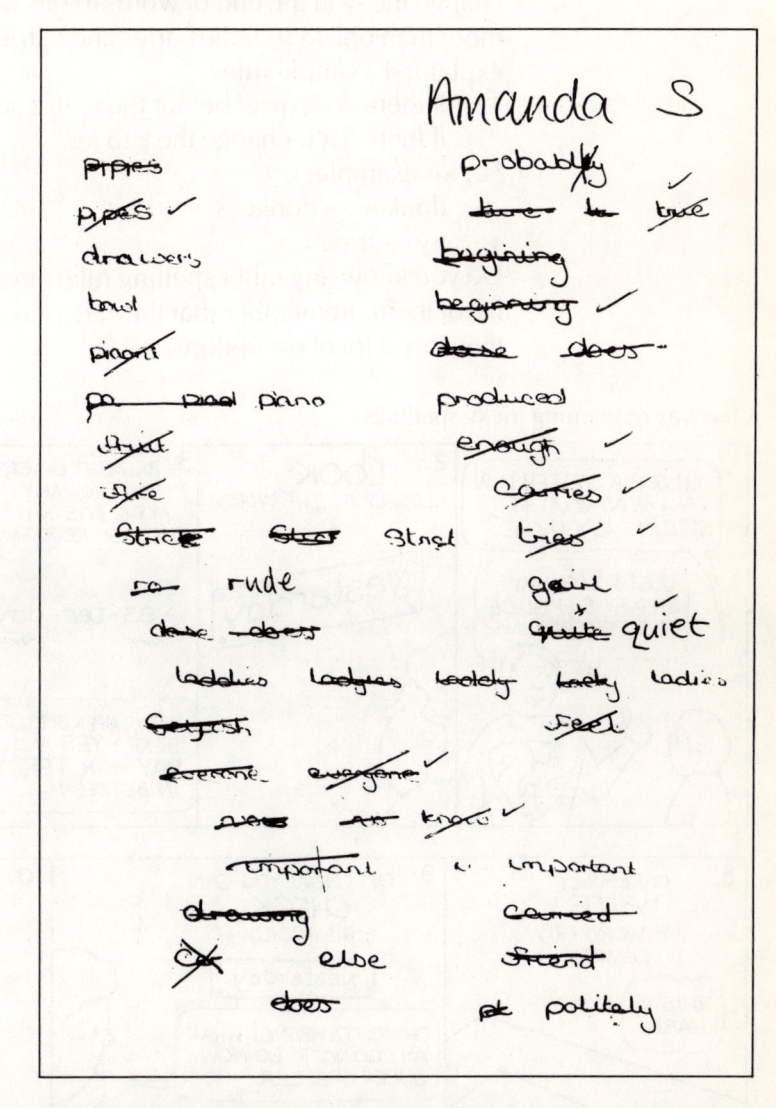

The spellings that are crossed off are the ones that Amanda eventually got right. She still has some to learn.

It is useful for your teacher to see a list of the spellings you find difficult.

Writing for yourself

Watch out for common errors

When you have a full sheet of spellings, look carefully at them. Do you see any mistakes you have made more than once?

You can see from Amanda's list that she often forgets to change the -*y* at the end of words to -*ies* when she means more than one (e.g. lad*ies*, tr*ies* and carr*ies*). Her teacher explained a simple rule:

If there is a vowel before the *y*, just add *s*;
if there isn't, change the *y* to *ies*.

So, for example:

donkey → donkey*s*
try → tr*ies*

Do you know any other spelling rules? In a group, make a list of them. Remember that they are only rough guides – there are a lot of exceptions.

One way of learning tricky spellings

1. OH, SUPER SPELLER, HOW CAN I BE AS GOOD AT SPELLING AS YOU ARE?
JUST FOLLOW MY STEP-BY-STEP GUIDE TO SUPER SPELLING

2. LOOK CLOSELY AT THE WORD
yesterday

3. BREAK IT UP. CAN YOU FIND ANY MORE BITS IN IT THAT YOU RECOGNIZE
yes-ter-day
WOW, SUPER SPELLER! THERE'S YES AND DAY WITH TER IN BETWEEN!

4. UNDERLINE THE PART YOU HAVE TROUBLE WITH
yesterday

8. CAREFULLY WRITE THE WORD FROM MEMORY
THIS IS HARD
yest

9. OK. NOW YOU CAN CHECK THE WORD
yesterday
OH NO, IT'S WRONG! WHAT AM I GOING TO DO NOW, SUPER SPELLER?
yesteday

10. DON'T WORRY, SUPER SPELLER IS STILL HERE.
JUST GO BACK AND TRY AGAIN

Memorise the most difficult spellings

Sometimes spellings are stubborn and refuse to be learnt. In this case you have to memorise them. The cartoon below shows one method we have found useful for remembering tricky spellings.

Learn useful spellings

The first spellings to learn are those you use in your everyday work. Your teachers probably point out spelling errors for you, anyway. Your parents or friends may help you to pick out mistakes by underlining them. Then you can have another go at getting the spelling right, and ask them to help you in the way suggested above.

5. NOW THIS IS THE BAD MOMENT. **COVER** UP THE WORD
[CENSORED]

6. NOW CLOSE YOUR EYES AND **REMEMBER** WHAT IT LOOKS LIKE
yesterday

7. SPELL IT IN THE AIR WITH YOUR HAND
yest...

11. LATER..... RIGHT!
yesterday
THANKS, SUPER SPELLER, THAT'S GREAT!

12. STEADY ON! WRITE IT AGAIN AND AGAIN TO MAKE SURE
yesterday
yesterday
yesterday

13. AND USE IT SOON IN YOUR WORK
Yesterday Super Speller taught me how to help improve my spelling.

14. SO ALWAYS...,
**LOOK
COVER
REMEMBER
WRITE**

Writing for yourself

Finding inspiration

This section suggests ways of finding inspiration by:
- ☐ making use of other people
- ☐ brainstorming for ideas
- ☐ keeping notes and jottings

All writers, even those who write to earn a living, may have trouble finding good ideas. Sometimes, they think they've found a good idea but then get stuck or bored.

Here is some advice we have found useful in this situation. Some of the suggestions involve other people — teachers, friends, family, classmates — who can provide help and ideas.

Make a list

Pour out a list of all the tiny details in your head about the subject in hand. Include any words, phrases or associations that pop into your mind, however strange they may be. This list might help later with the detailed writing. It may also alert you to unusual or interesting angles.

DESERTED HOUSE

banquet – decaying food.
candelabra
cobwebs everywhere
portraits on way – stern, looking down, disapproving
velvet cushions on chairs
goblets
darkness
mice, spiders, scuttling sounds
nibbling at food

Finding inspiration

Brainstorming

Give other people your topic. Then ask them for suggestions. Brainstorm for a short period (about 3 minutes). Jot down *all* of the ideas as they come. At this stage don't worry about whether the ideas seem useful, just concentrate on catching passing thoughts which might turn into good ideas later. Keep your notes brief. Don't try to develop them at this stage.

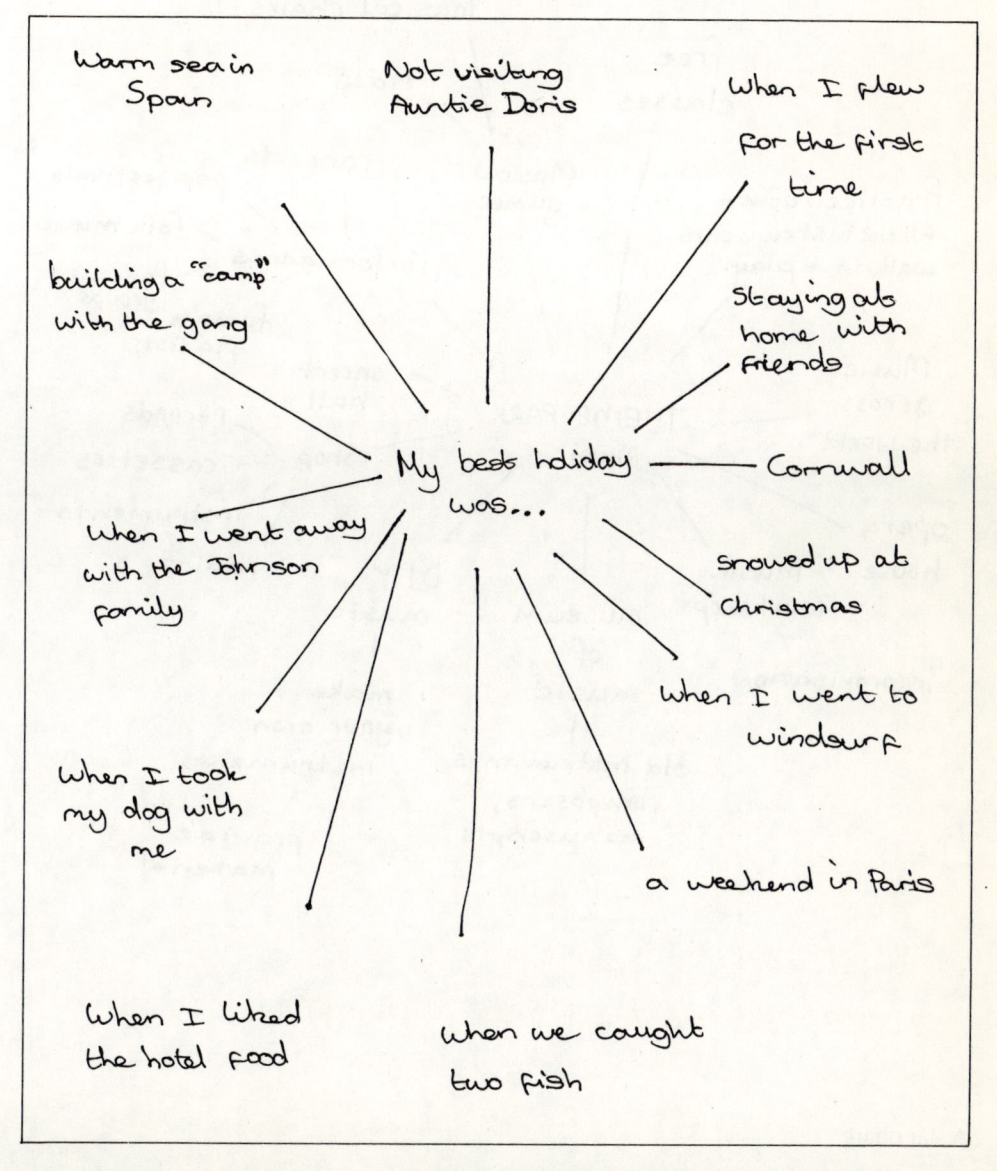

- Warm sea in Spain
- Not visiting Auntie Doris
- When I flew for the first time
- building a "camp" with the gang
- Staying at home with friends
- My best holiday was...
- Cornwall
- When I went away with the Johnson family
- snowed up at Christmas
- When I took my dog with me
- When I went to windsurf
- a weekend in Paris
- When I liked the hotel food
- when we caught two fish

Writing for yourself

Map out your subject

Lay out your ideas in the form of a diagram.

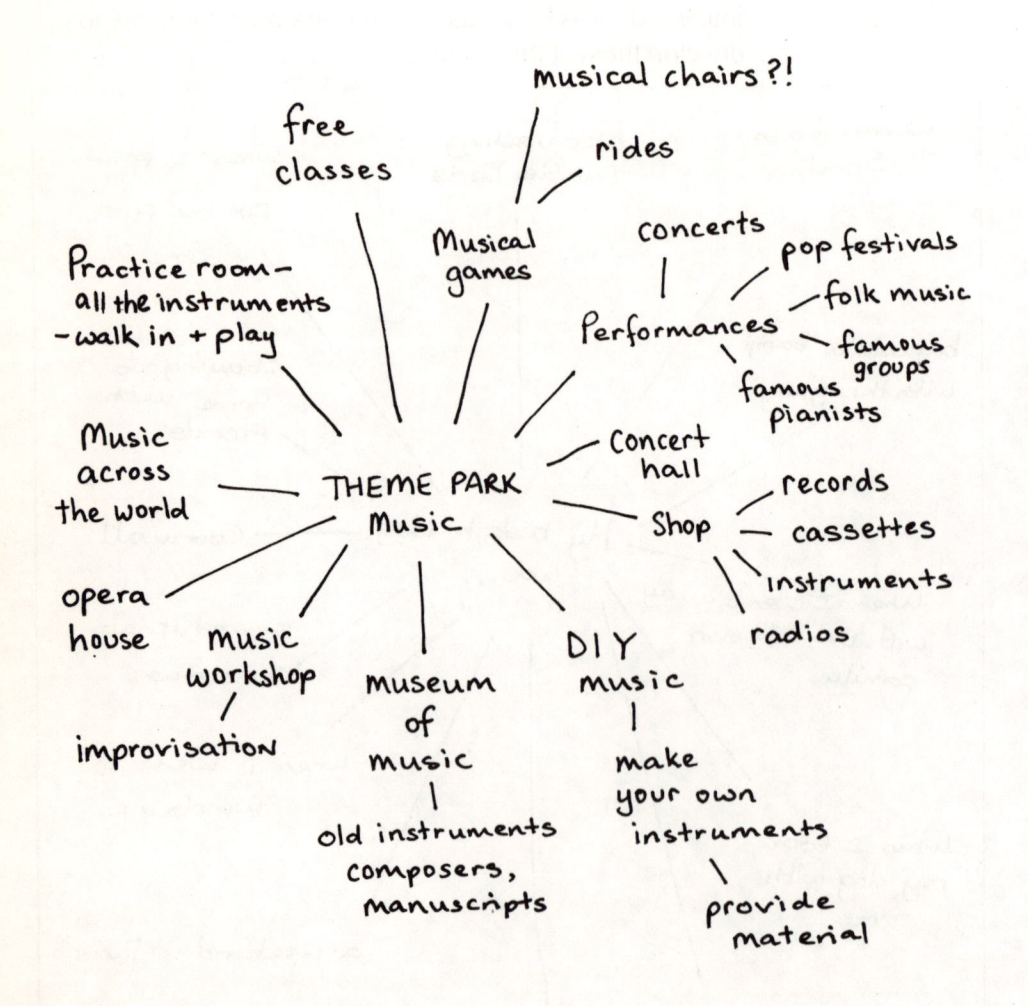

- free classes
- musical chairs?!
- rides
- Musical games
- concerts
- pop festivals
- folk music
- Practice room — all the instruments — walk in + play
- Performances
- famous groups
- famous pianists
- Music across the world
- THEME PARK Music
- Concert hall
- Shop
- records
- cassettes
- instruments
- radios
- opera house
- music workshop
- improvisation
- museum of music
- old instruments composers, manuscripts
- DIY music
- make your own instruments
- provide material

A star chart

Finding inspiration

MAKING A TELEPHONE CALL FROM A CALL BOX

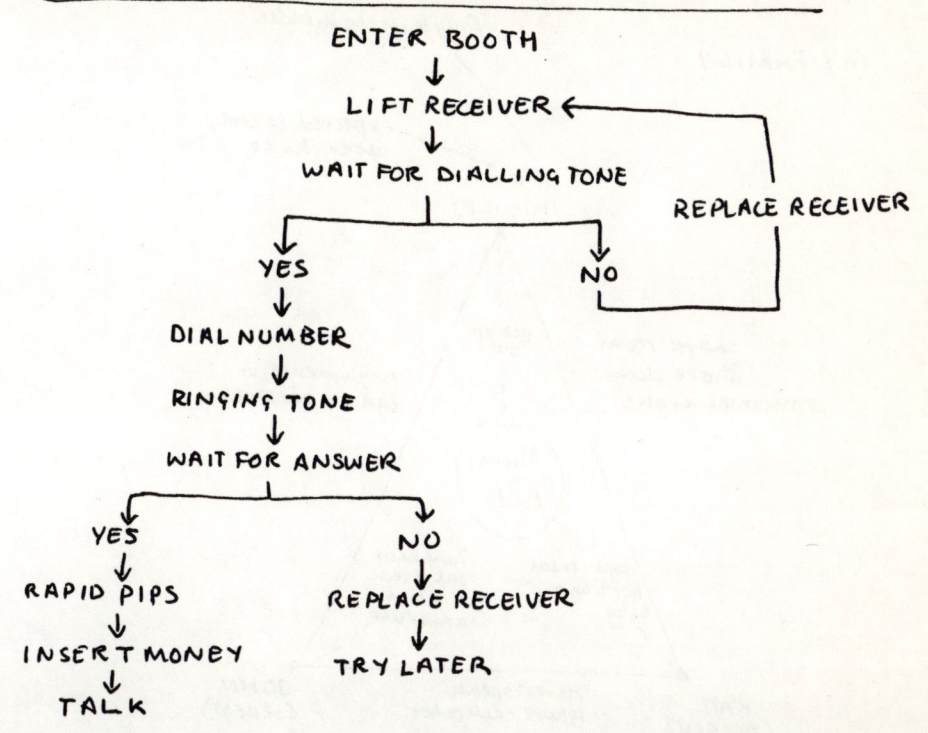

ENTER BOOTH
↓
LIFT RECEIVER ←
↓
WAIT FOR DIALLING TONE
↓
YES / NO
- YES ↓ DIAL NUMBER ↓ RINGING TONE ↓ WAIT FOR ANSWER
  - YES ↓ RAPID PIPS ↓ INSERT MONEY ↓ TALK
  - NO ↓ REPLACE RECEIVER ↓ TRY LATER
- NO → REPLACE RECEIVER

A flow chart

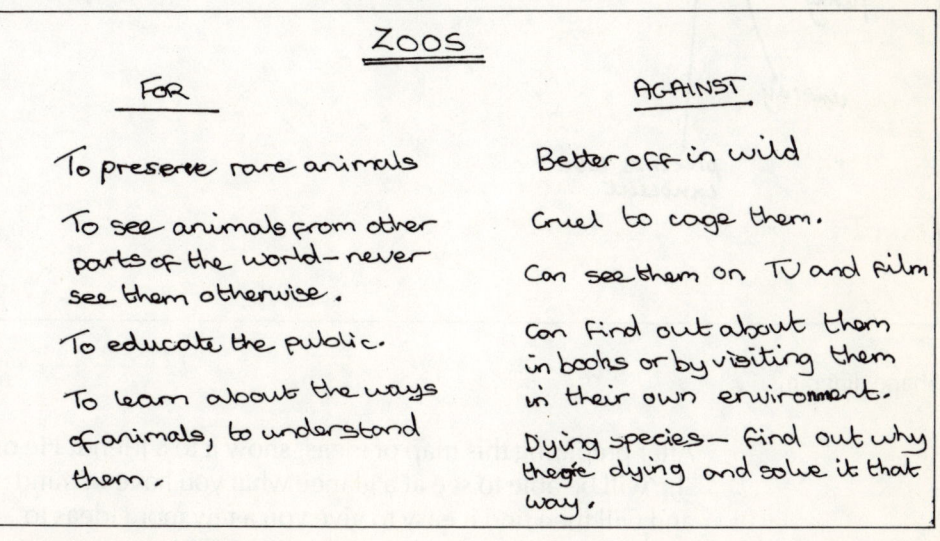

ZOOS

FOR	AGAINST
To preserve rare animals	Better off in wild
To see animals from other parts of the world — never see them otherwise.	Cruel to cage them.
To educate the public.	Can see them on TV and film
To learn about the ways of animals, to understand them.	Can find out about them in books or by visiting them in their own environment.
	Dying species — find out why they're dying and solve it that way.

'For' and 'against' columns

Writing for yourself

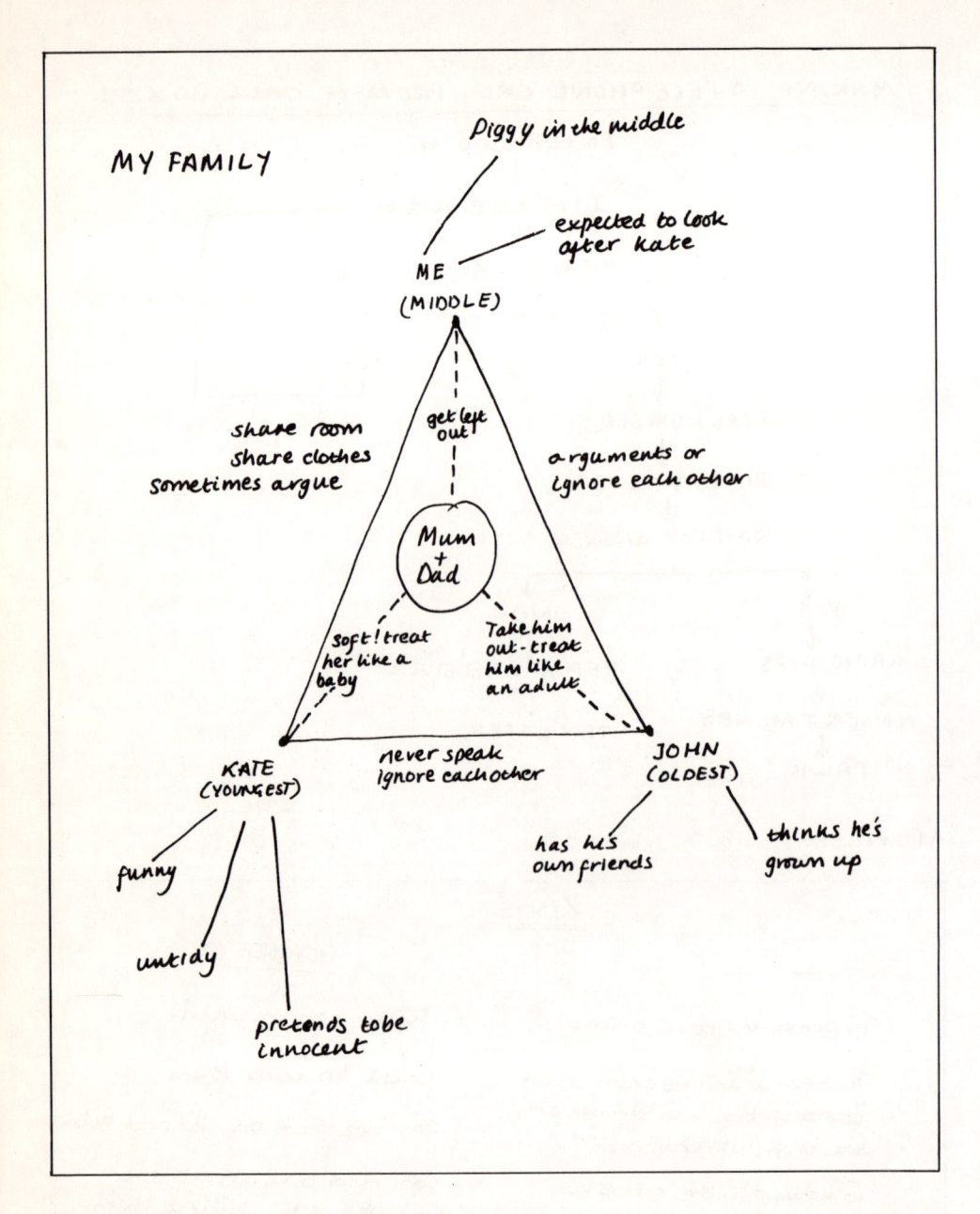

MY FAMILY

- Piggy in the middle
- expected to look after Kate

ME (MIDDLE)

- get left out

share room
share clothes
sometimes argue

arguments or ignore each other

Mum + Dad

Soft! treat her like a baby

Take him out - treat him like an adult

KATE (YOUNGEST) — never speak ignore each other — JOHN (OLDEST)

- funny
- untidy
- pretends to be innocent

- has his own friends
- thinks he's grown up

Shape diagrams

After preparing this map of ideas, show it to a friend. He or she will be able to see at a glance what you have in mind and will then find it easy to give you a few more ideas to add in.

Finding inspiration

Force yourself to write

Set yourself a time limit – say 4 minutes – and start writing. *You must not stop until the time is up.* Just keep going, even if you're not happy with it. Most people find that a bit of what they write is useful and provides a starting point for more ideas.

> The best cat I ever had was Ginger. He was real fun. My Mum said he was 'a character.' His best trick was jumping off the kitchen roof onto your shoulders as you went past. It gave you a real shock...

You have to be prepared to reject most of what you write, in the hope that a small part of it will be good enough to set you going.

Writing for yourself

Improving work

This section contains advice about:
- [ ] self-help
- [ ] making good use of available help
- [ ] learning from your mistakes

General advice

Experience has proved to us that the best writers help themselves by following some simple guidelines:
- Write often. The more writing you do, the better you become at it. (See the section on 'Keeping a diary'.)
- Where there is a choice, choose subjects you know about or enjoy.
- Write from personal experience, or at least base your writing on personal experience, wherever possible.
- Don't be unduly depressed by mistakes and negative comments – think about them and learn from them.
- Seek advice, especially before your work is finished. This is not cheating. Use other people to get ideas, comments and help before it's too late. Don't let them do the work for you – you won't improve that way – but do get them to point you in the direction of new ideas, or to make general criticisms.
- Don't expect to write the perfect piece of work first time round. Occasionally, put aside the time to write a draft and then to improve it.

Drafting

If you write a draft, you can concentrate on getting all your ideas onto paper: you need not worry about neatness and accuracy until later on. In the meantime, you will be able to improve the work. It sometimes helps to leave the work on one side for a while, and then to re-read it with fresh eyes. It also helps to show it to other people for general comments.

Here, for example, is the first draft of a piece of writing by Hilary. She was asked to write about a personal experience she had when she was on holiday in France. This is her first opening:

Improving your work

> ~~A French Mountain Lake~~
>
> It was a beautiful place, so quiet, so peaceful. The gentle ~~~~ mountain sunlight glittering on the ~~lake gentle~~ ripples of the lake. The ~~silence~~ of the morning only broken by the piercing ~~screech~~ cry of an eagle flying high above the pine forests, ~~circling its prey~~ circled, hovered ~~and made its first descent.~~

Hilary's first draft

You can that see she was unhappy with it and crossed it out. The small changes she started off with were not enough. She started again:

> It was a beautiful place, so quiet, so peaceful. The gentle rays of mountain sunlight reflecting on ~~off~~ the quiet waters of the lake. The ~~~~ silence of the morning ^only broken ~~only~~ by the gentle sound of the rippling water and the faint cry of an eagle. I looked up and far above the lake and ~~~~ pine forests I saw an ~~majestic~~ bird circling and hovering about to dive and ~~attack~~ its prey.
>
> We had found this mountain lake only a few days ago ~~after driving~~ it was about an hours drive from our little french farmhouse where we were staying

Hilary's second draft

Hilary was more satisfied with this version, and the writing started to flow. She felt able to go on and get into her story. But she still went back to change a few words and to add in new ones.

25

Writing for yourself

After she had written the essay in this way, she went back and wrote it all out neatly and correctly:

Tragedy at Lac Jenin.

It was a beautiful place, so quiet, so peaceful. The gentle rays of mountain sunlight reflecting on the quiet waters of the lake. The silence of the morning broken only by the gentle sound of the rippling water and the faint cry of an eagle. I looked up and far above the lake and pine forests I saw a bird circling and hovering, about to dive and attack its prey.

We had found this mountain lake only a few days ago. It was about an hour's drive from our little French farmhouse where we were staying.

Hilary's final version

How to improve a draft

Hilary, whose work you have just read, explains how she goes about writing her drafts:

When I am doing a piece of writing I like to do a rough draft first. When writing in rough I do a lot of crossing out and changing words. As I write every few sentences, I go back and read over what I have just written and make any appropriate changes. If the piece of writing is long, it takes me several lessons. At the beginning of every lesson I go back and read what I did in the previous one and check over my work. Sometimes I read back from the beginning just to check that everything flows smoothly. Occasionally I read my rough work out loud so that I can hear how the words go together. When I write it out in neat, I change words around as I write, and sometimes I move paragraphs around.

HILARY

Sue goes about it differently:

I write my first draft really quickly. It looks awful! It's untidy, there are lots of mistakes in it, and some bits are just nonsense. On the other hand, a lot of it is good, and I sometimes think 'I didn't know I could write like that!' Although it looks scruffy and I don't use a lot of it, there are always a few good ideas and even some long bits which are just right as they are. It is very quick. I then spend all the time I have left to re-write it. I cut out a lot and change a lot. My neat work doesn't often look like my first draft.

SUE

Michael says:

I never write more than one draft. I write a sentence and then I correct it until it's just right. I do most of my drafting in my head before I put it on paper. I write very slowly and neatly, and some of my teachers think I am too slow or lazy, but all the time I am thinking, getting it right in my head. I can't stand my work being untidy. I like to get it right as I go along.

MICHAEL

Writing for yourself

Another student, Sarah, wrote a draft for a review of Noel Streatfield's book, *White Boots*:

> The main characters in "White Boots" are Harriet, ~~Lalla~~ Lalla, ~~Nana~~ A.C. and Olivia. H & L are two completely different ~~characters~~ children ~~One~~ Harriet is poor and delicate whilst ~~Lalla the other~~ is confident, rich and a show off sometimes. ~~Harriet is a thin~~
>
> ⇒ The 1st paragraph in the story describes H as "a thin child with big brown eyes & a lot of reddish hair."

There are a number of mistakes and crossings-out, but these do not matter because this is only a draft. The changes show that Sarah is thinking about her work and improving it:

> The main characters in "White Boots" are Harriet and her mother Olivia Johnson, Lalla and her Aunt Claudia. Harriet and Lalla are two girls who are different in every way. Harriet is delicate and nervous whilst Lalla is confident, rich and sometimes a show off.
>
> Harriet is first described as a "thin child with big brown eyes and a lot of reddish hair."

Writing a draft makes more sense than waiting for the teacher to tell you what is wrong. Mark your own work. The ability to see problems and improve your writing comes with practice.

Here are some things you can do with a draft:
- ☐ change words
- ☐ move bits around
- ☐ cut out the bad bits
- ☐ add in new bits
- ☐ show it to other people for comments
- ☐ throw it away if it's no good
- ☐ experiment with ideas
- ☐ check spellings and punctuation

If you have access to a word-processor in your school, you can do these things on a screen without all the bother of re-writing. You can change and correct the writing as you go along. Some people find writing by hand too slow for their ideas – they can write more quickly with a word-processor. Others, whose ideas soon dry up, find that they can write more on a word-processor. And some people, who become frustrated with their own untidy handwriting and poor spelling, like the neat appearance of text printed by the word-processor. They don't mind having to change spellings if they don't have to re-write everything. Some word-processors will even check your spelling for you!

Learn from your mistakes

Get out a few pieces of marked work, and make a list of all the signs and symbols your teacher uses in marking. Next to each one, write what you think the teacher means by it. For example:

Sp = spelling mistake
// = start a new paragraph

Check with your teacher that you have understood all the marks, and ask the meaning of any you do not understand.

What do you do with returned work? Do you:
- ☐ just look at the mark?
- ☐ compare your mark with those of other people?
- ☐ just read the comments at the bottom?
- ☐ scan it to see how many mistakes you made?

Writing for yourself

All these things are interesting, but they will not help you to improve. What *should* you do? You should:
- try incorrect spellings again
- re-phrase bits the teacher said were unclear or dull
- reply to comments made or questions asked by the teacher — you could write in the margin or at the end
- re-write unsatisfactory parts, if you can find the time
- make any other improvements or corrections suggested in the marking

In this way you will learn to improve your work by helping yourself.

Presenting work

In this section you will find suggestions about:
- ☐ improving the appearance of written work
- ☐ making use of available equipment
- ☐ decorating your work

Attractive presentation is not simply a frill — something unimportant which just makes a piece of work look good. When you take pride in your work, the quality of what you say will improve too.

Choose a realistic format

If you are writing a diary, make it *look* as well as *read* like one. Make a booklet with stiff card covers.

If you are collecting poems for an anthology or if you are 'publishing' your short stories, make them into a book or collect them into a separate file or folder. The diagram opposite may give you some ideas.

Find original ways to present longer pieces of work

Your art teacher or craft, design and technology teacher might show you how to make a *book binding*. This involves clamping the pages together and using some rubber-based glue and cotton gauze to bind the book together. You can then cover this binding with coloured

Presenting work

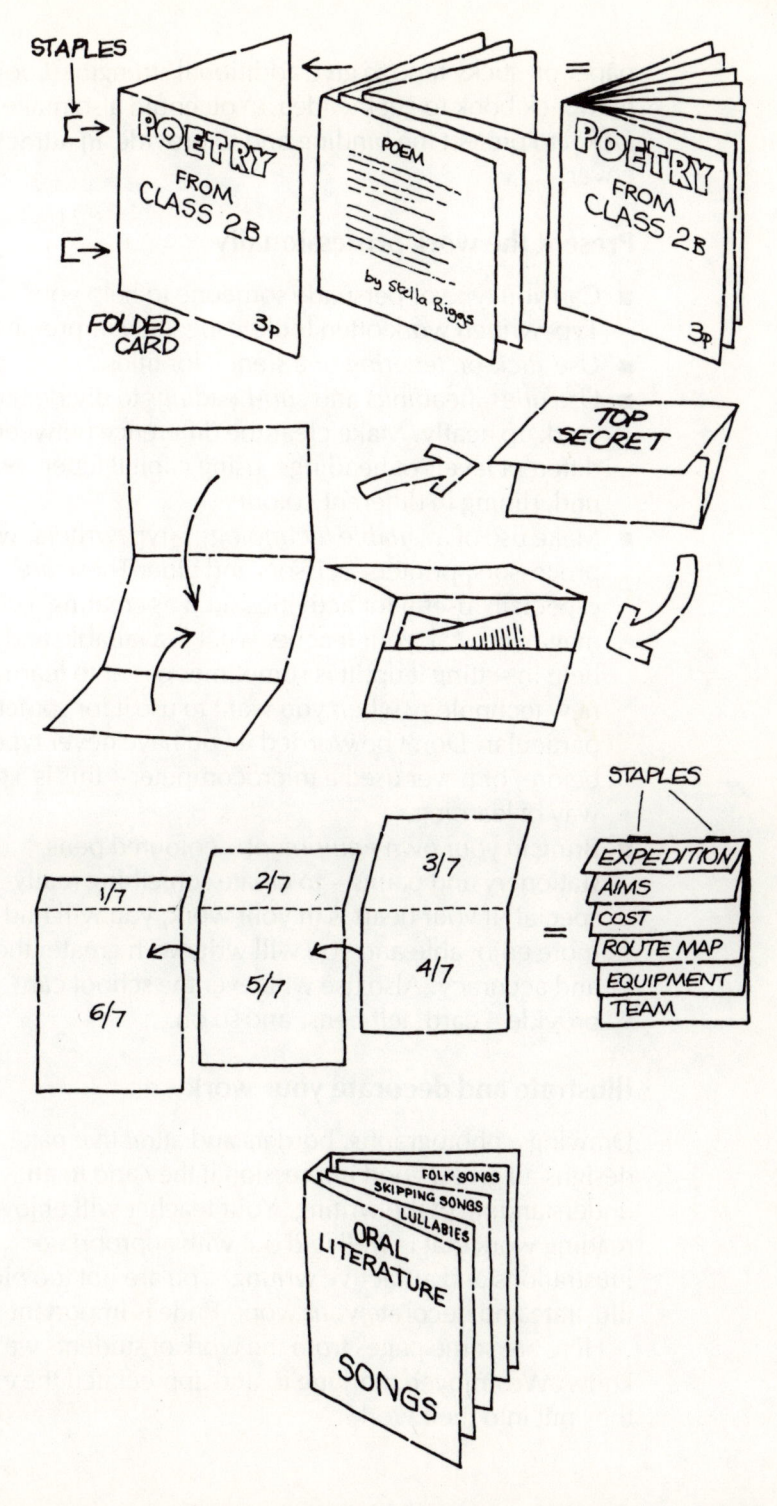

paper on sticky tape to give additional strength. (Look at a hardback book to get the idea.) You could also make a *dust jacket* to protect the binding and to provide an attractive cover.

Present the work professionally

- Can you *type* or persuade someone to help you? Typewritten work often looks especially impressive.
- Use *stick-on lettering* or a *stencil* for titles.
- Use *titles*, *headings* and *sub-headings* to divide the work up neatly. Make clear the difference between different levels of headings, using capital letters or underlining in different colours.
- Make use of *available technology* – typewriters, word-processors, printers, scissors and glue. These are especially useful for activities such as creating a class magazine. Ask your teacher what is available and for help in setting it up. It is sometimes easier to learn to use new technology when you want to use it for something particular. Don't be worried if you have never typed before, or never used a microcomputer – this is a good way of learning.
- Bring in *your own equipment* – coloured pens, stationery and paints – to create something really special. If your heart is in your work, you will find it more enjoyable and you will write with greater thought and accuracy. Also use whatever the school can provide – card, felt pens, and so on.

Illustrate and decorate your work

Drawings, photographs, borders and attractive page designs all give a good impression if they add to an understanding of the writing. Your teacher will enjoy reading work that is well laid out with appropriate illustrations and attractive writing. You are not too old to illustrate and decorate your work. Pride is important.

Here are some pages from the work of students we know. We enjoyed marking it, and appreciated the effort they put into their work.

SURVIVAL

PROTECTION IS NEEDED FROM THE ELEMENTS AND FROM WILD ANIMALS ETC. IN A STORM TRY TO SHELTER IN DENSE WOODLAND OR UNDER THE FOOT OF A STEEP/OVER HANGING CLIFF. USE ANY AVAILABLE MATERIALS TO BUILD A REFUGE. HERE ARE A FEW BASIC SHELTERS :-

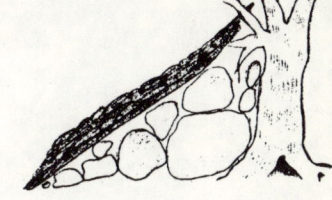

| 2 SHELTER |
| 3 FOOD |
| 4 WARMTH |
| 5 FIRST AID |
| 6 HELP |

Graham (also pages 34–7)

Writing for yourself

Mem Strang is the Colonel's lady and in comparison to Marjorie she is regarded with more respect by others. Mrs. Strang is a kind hearted lady and a good wife: 'I thought you were feeling a little tired, Colonel dear. ... No, no, don't get up.... I'd forgive you anything.' Although the part of Mem is not a 'great character' part the continuous affection she shows towards everyone, and especially the Colonel must be made clear from the first words she speaks in the scene. Mem also has a sense of duty to socialise and it becomes apparent that she has been with the Colonel little during the Ball: 'All evening I have danced with bounding young men and doddering old bones. I should so like to dance with my own dear husband.' This warmness and affection is carried through into the situation when Mrs. Hasseltine appears on the veranda: 'It's all right, it's all right, it's all right.' Mem is one of the few people to actually help Mrs. Hasseltine, and the repetition of 'it's all right' acts to calm Marjorie down from her state of panic. (A stroking of Marjorie's forehead or hand by Mem may be appropriate here.) Mem's affection leads to concern for Mrs. Hasseltine: 'Give me a hand, will you, Alistair, lift her....' Although it is the Colonel who orders the brandy, Pradah Singh gives it to Mem — she is the closest person to Marjorie (kneeling next to her?) When Mem says 'She's been attacked, Doctor' her thoughts are for the welfare of Mrs Hasseltine and not for the immidiate capture of the attacker, like many of the men: Wimbourne: 'Who? That's what I want to know! Who did it?' Marjorie is in a great deal of stress and it appears that only a few people, other than herself, are more concerned about her than the culprit.

CATCHPHRASES/ORDERS

This section of the booklet deals with the subject you will probably encounter most — Catchphrases and orders.
Here is a list of some with their meanings:

1. Get fell in — Stand in rank and line.
2. Attention — Not 'pay attention' but feet together, arms at your sides.
3. At Ease — Feet apart, hands crossed behind back.
4. Halt! — Stop
5. A point — That you shout when you have stuck the stuffed boar during a game of 'Sticking the Pig'.
6. A chukka — A period of time in a match of polo.
7. a 'fait accompli' — a situation where one is forced to do something.
8. joie de vivre' — The joy of life/living.
9. 'sahib' — Indian way of saying 'Sir'.
10. 'mem sahib' — Indian way of saying 'Madam'.
11. Thrashing the pants off them — beating them (in a game).
12. gel — girl servant/maid.
13. damned fine game — 'damned' is used instead of 'very' to sound emphatic.

REGIMENTAL HONOUR

he honour of the Regiment should be the most
ortant thing to you. Centuries of pride and
dition have aided its progression to the fine
tion of the Army it is today.
ere are some points about Regimental honour.
 Colonel Strang is the most important and
mourable man in the Regiment.
 We have an unequalled record of three Victoria
Crosses.
 We have a hero, Captain Scarlett, who was
killed at Ratjahpur. His tunic is on display in
the m_____ t__ room _____ full mess dress ___
It is
mea
Bein
polo
To d
Fi
you
tin

THE UNOFFICIAL GUIDE

IN ARDUIS FIDELIS

TO THE REGIMENT

PULL-OUT LEAFLET ON MESS DRESS INSIDE

Writing for yourself

My friends number zero, my acquaintances, perhaps twenty. I am not all that popular because I resent fitting into the typical teenage stereotype image. I'm no rebel, but I find the face/boys/disco syndrome boring. I will accommodate, agree, fit in and follow to become inconspicuous and unobtrusive. I do not follow fashion, I follow myself. I am ambitious, but perseverance and patience are not my strong points. I have a hot temper and do not possess a cool, calm collected outlook on life. I'm quite witty in a sarcastic manner. I like caustic, subtle and wry humour. My hobbies are the solitary pursuits of reading and writing poetry. I play the clarinet which I enjoy, and I love going to the theatre.

Rachel: *Myself*

Presenting work

> I HATE THIS PERSON AND SHE HATES ME SO WE GET ON REALLY WELL. I LIE WITH MY NOSE UNDER THE FENCE WAITING FOR HER TO COME HOME FROM SCHOOL. SHE WALKS UP THE ROAD STRAIGHT TOWARDS ME. I START GROWLING AS SOON AS I SEE HER. WHEN SHE'S GETTING CLOSER I START BARING MY FANGS THEN AS SHE REACHES THE GATE I GO MAD BARKING AND HOWLING, IT SCARES THE LIVING DAYLIGHTS OUT OF HER. I LOVE IT! IT'S GREAT FUN. IF SHE SETS ONE FOOT IN THE GARDEN TO FETCH 'THAT STUPID FRISBEE THING', I SINK MY TEETH INTO IT (OR HER IF POSSIBLE) WE HAVE GREAT FUN, IT'S A RELATIONSHIP BUILT ON FEAR!!

Rachel: *My dog's opinion of me*

Writing for yourself

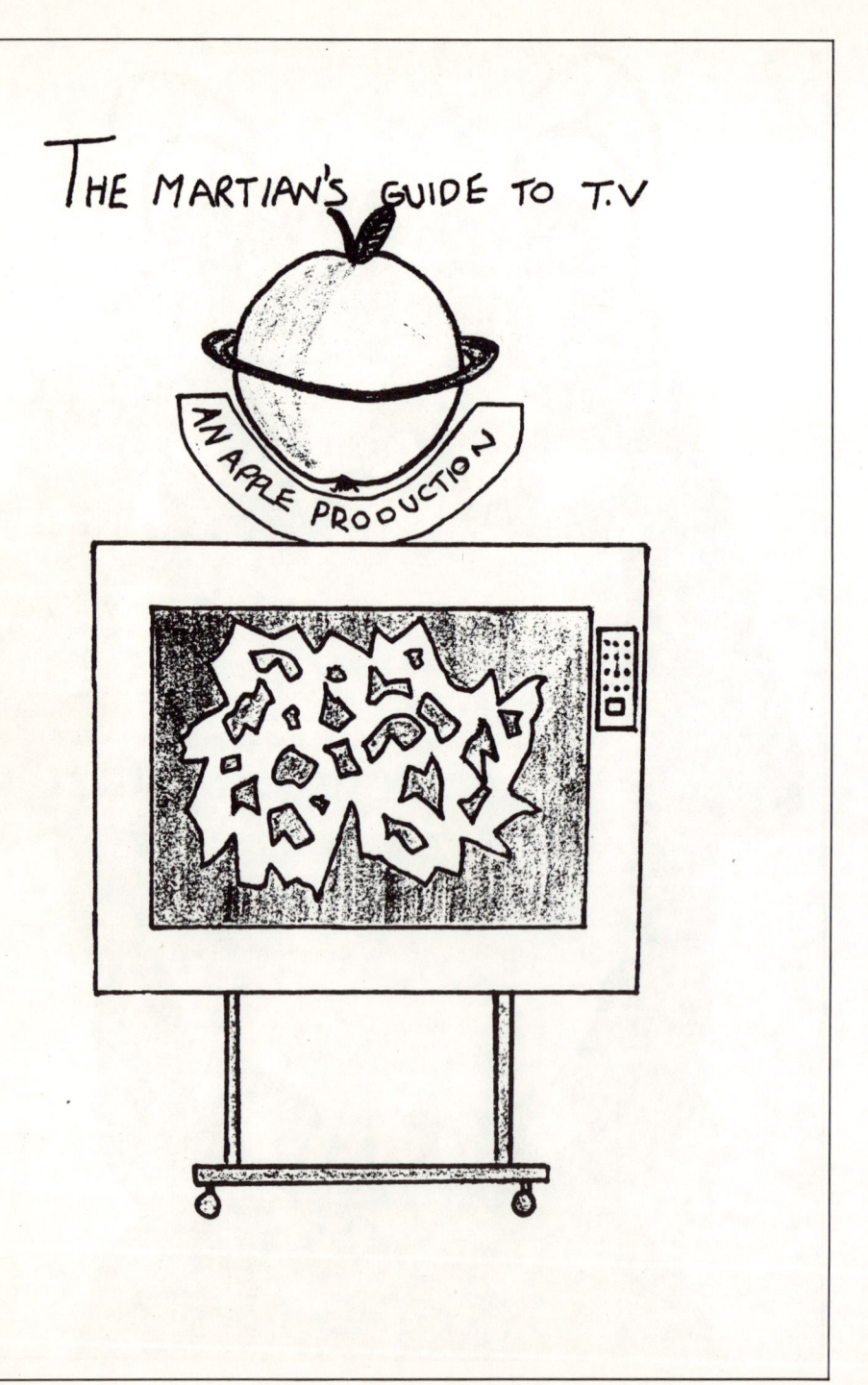

Steven

2 Picture this

Close your eyes – and see pictures. Imagine a new face . . . a different room . . . life on another planet. You can probably see pictures with your mind's eye even with your eyes open, as you do when you think, daydream or remember. You even see pictures in your dreams. Everyone makes images like these – we are all using our imaginations.

Good writers and good readers have active imaginations. They continually see pictures in their minds, especially of the things they write and read about.

This chapter encourages you to exercise your imagination as you write.

Picture words

This activity encourages:
- originality
- thoughtful presentation
- an awareness of words and their meanings

These words have been written in ways that illustrate their meanings:

ALON   E   SHRINk

JBDUMEL   BOUNCE

mis$ta¢kes

Picture this

How would you draw these words?
- ☐ growing
- ☐ balloon
- ☐ looking
- ☐ mirror
- ☐ illegible

Now try drawing some words of your own. Here are some examples by other students:

FALL — Debbie

REFLECTIONS / REFLECTIONS (mirrored) — Debbie

flowers — Sally-Anne

DO$$AR — Camilla

(spider/web design) — Jess — TO

SAINT — Rachel

chain — Rachel

L♥VE — Camilla

— Gabrielle

CUP➤•

Education AD 3000

This activity should encourage:
- ☐ an ambitious imagination
- ☐ a sense of humour
- ☐ a sense of audience

It is the year AD 3000.
- ■ Imagine education: how will it be then?
- ■ Which subjects will be taught and how?
- ■ Who will learn and who will teach?

Education AD 3000

Imagine you are a student in the year AD 3000.
- Write your *timetable*.
- Draw a labelled *map* of your school or college, showing special facilities and interesting features.
- Describe a typical *lesson* in one of your more unusual subjects.
- Design a *leaflet* for new students, explaining the aims, organisation and teaching methods of your school or college.

One of your subjects in the year AD 3000 is history. One day, you learn about the schools that existed way back in the twentieth century. For homework, you are asked to explain what has become of some of the ancient institutions:
- ☐ the headteacher
- ☐ school dinners
- ☐ morning assembly
- ☐ the cane
- ☐ the form tutor
- ☐ examinations

Write your homework.

During another history lesson you go on a day trip to visit the ruins of a school or college – the one you are attending

Picture this

now. Write an account of this visit, saying what you found interesting, amusing and even surprising about the primitive education endured by students in the twentieth century.

Here is an extract from the work of Amanda, who wrote about the Xenon Education Centre:

A GUIDE TO THE XENON EDUCATION CENTRE

First Day

On arriving at Xenon Education Centre you will be shown where to go by an android who will meet you as you enter the main passage. Give him your name and he will issue you with an identification bracelet which must be worn at all times until discharge day.

The android will direct you to the lecture station where the Master will welcome you on program 356825. Please ensure that you remember this data so you can reprogram it later. After the initial welcome you will be introduced to your Group Leader. The importance and role of your Group Leader will be explained clearly as you spend the rest of the morning in his or her care.

At Refuelling Hour, you must report to the Food Station for your "vita-pack" which must be eaten in the Hall. Anyone found eating outside the Station will be duly punished.

In the afternoon, report back to your Group Leader who will introduce you to your personal tutor. These computers have been specially programmed to help you learn as much as possible and they provide you will all the help you need. You will be expected to look after your unit with the utmost care and if anything goes wrong, or gets broken, you are responsible.

Your tutor will issue you with a timetable and any further information you require. On your first day you will receive no Preparatory Studies so you may leave the Centre at 1600 hours. Usually you must remain until 1700 hours to prepare your lessons for the following day as instructed by your tutor.

The deserted house

This story requires:
- ☐ a vivid imagination
- ☐ a detailed description
- ☐ a sense of atmosphere

45

During a walk in a remote part of the country, you come across a large house. The grounds are neglected and overgrown. It is clear that the place is deserted and has been for many years. A sudden downpour has you scurrying for cover in the porch. You notice that the door is slightly ajar. The rain is beating down, and you decide to enter the house and explore.

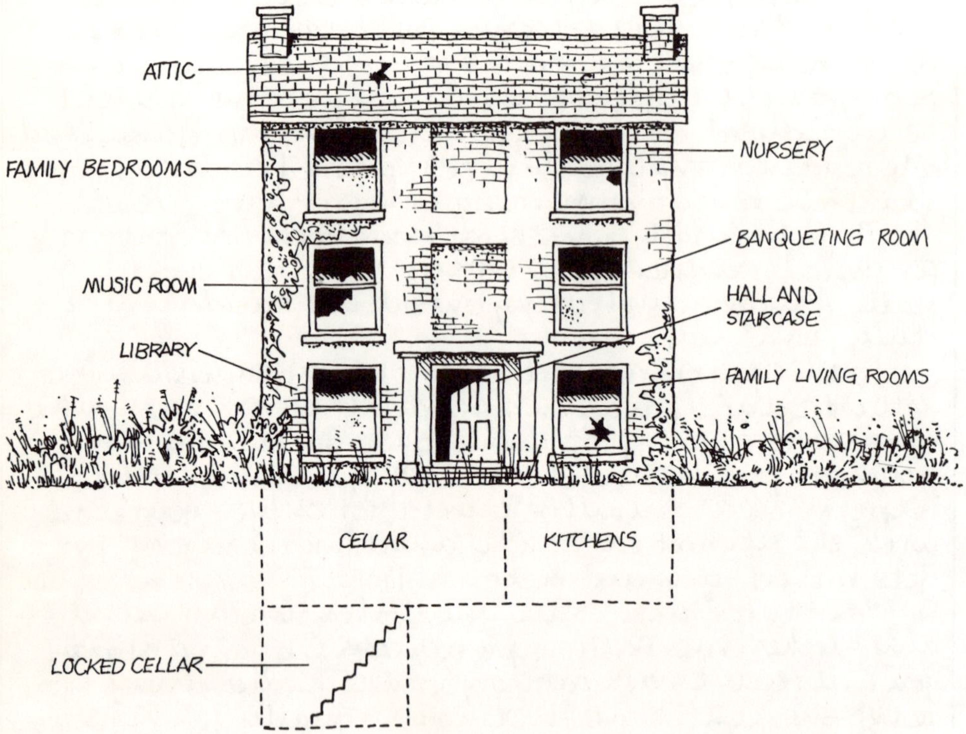

Using this plan, or a plan of your own, describe what you see as you enter, and give an account of your exploration.

Cartoon strips

This is an exercise in:

- ☐ telling a story simply and dramatically
- ☐ using words economically
- ☐ matching words and pictures

Cartoon strips

Cartoons are very popular. Collect examples of cartoon strips and discuss your favourite stories and characters. What do you consider to be the ingredients of a successful cartoon?

Terry created this cartoon strip:

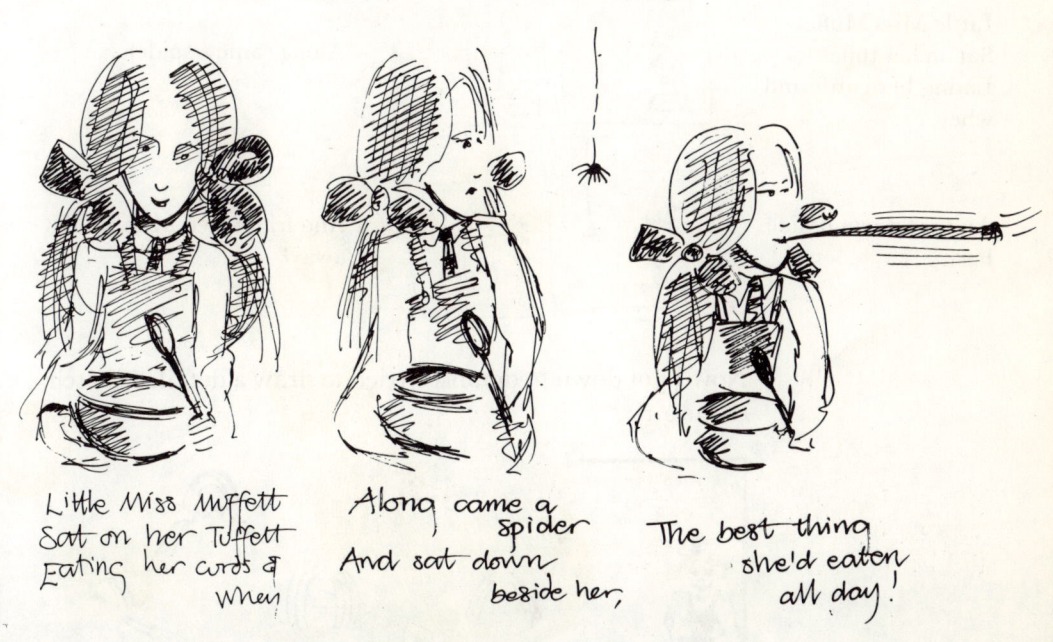

Little Miss Muffett
Sat on her Tuffett
Eating her curds &
whey

Along came a spider
And sat down beside her,

The best thing she'd eaten all day!

Before he began, he experimented with words and pictures like this:

At first, I was experimenting with the idea of a man with a leaky umbrella, but I could not visualise him. Then I drew a girl and changed my idea. I had no words in my head at all at this stage.

47

Picture this

The girl reminded me of Little Miss Muffet in the nursery rhyme, and I thought I might use the words. I wrote out the rhyme and tried to draw the actions in four boxes:

Little Miss Muffet
Sat on her tuffet
Eating her curds and
whey . . .

Along came a spider . . .

And sat down beside her . . .

And frightened Miss Muffet away!

Now I got down to details. I tried to draw a detailed sketch of the girl:

Finally I chose this one:

And I started to draw the sequence of actions in the nursery rhyme. I was wondering how to make a joke of it, how to make it amusing. I thought of changing the last line.

48

Cartoon strips

I spent a lot of time on the 'punchline' picture.

When I came to draw the final sequence, I realised I could do it in three steps. This was what I ended up with:

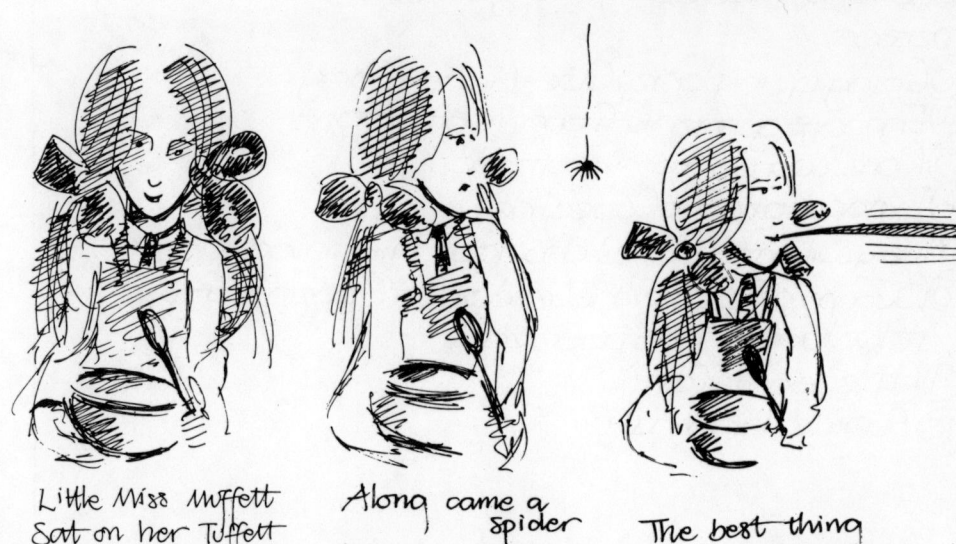

Little Miss Muffett Sat on her Tuffett Eating her curds & whey

Along came a spider And sat down beside her,

The best thing she'd eaten all day!

Terry

Picture this

This student, by contrast, planned his cartoon in writing and then drew it. These are his notes:

Fighting: reason for fight. Type of fighting between who. Numbers involved. Who finally wins.

Smoking: For or against it. Those who make up the story. Encouragement from others. Final result.

Parachute: Get to plane. Others involved. Feeling. Encouragement. What finally happens. Parachutist's own thoughts.

Walking, rowing, dreaming, racing.

1) Encouragement and person's feeling.
2) (Full of enthusiasm) A very doubtful and unwilling person
3) Going up in plane. Questions, if any?
4) Encouragement from instructor?
5) More words from instructor.
6) Exaggeration of weather.
7) (Very willing to jump) changed his mind
8) (Jumps and parachute doesn't open) very reluctant and is pushed.
9) A pleasant fall?
10) A nice landing?

And here is part of his cartoon:

Cartoon strips

Parachuting's Fun

1. "Go on you coward, there is nothing to it!" "It'll be great. Just great." "Today's my first parachute jump. God I hope it's called off."

2. PARACHUTE 1 "Have you checked the weather, it looks like rain?" "Yes! Just get on board"

3. "How high are we going? And what about those clouds?" "We are going another five thousand feet, and the weather is perfectly safe."

4. "Right, this is high enough. Get out." "And what country shall I land in?"

5. "This is your stop, hurry up and get out"

6. RUMBLE! RUMBLE! BANG! BANG! CRASH!

Picture this

Finally, here is an original cartoon by Ruskin and David (aged 12) about the adventures of Gerald McGonk and his trusty friend, the hairy caterpillar.

Gerald is lost in a scary underground tunnel and encounters some rather unpleasant characters....

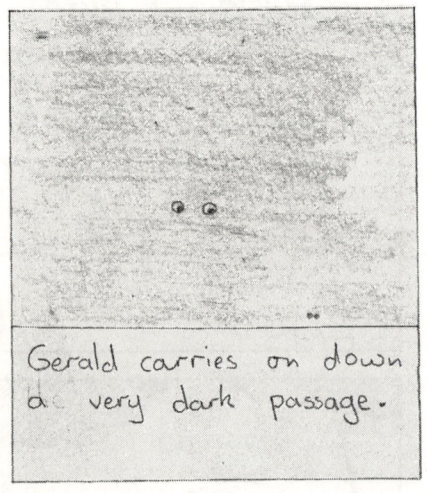

After a very fierce fight the spider lies on its back, Dead.

Gerald carries on down a very dark passage.

Gerald eventually comes out into a massive cave. Towering above him is a dragon. He starts praying.

Cartoon strips

Later on in the same story, Gerald and the hairy caterpillar fall through a trapdoor into a mysterious chamber....

Gerald and his hairy caterpillar hit the ground with a great thump!

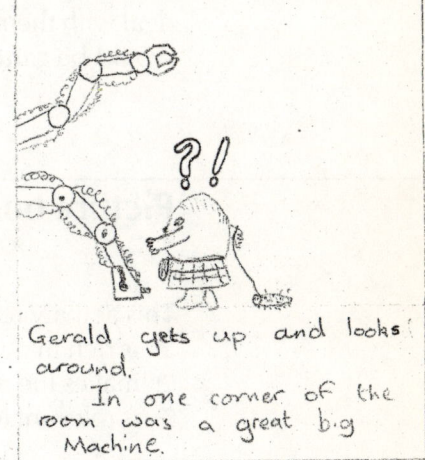

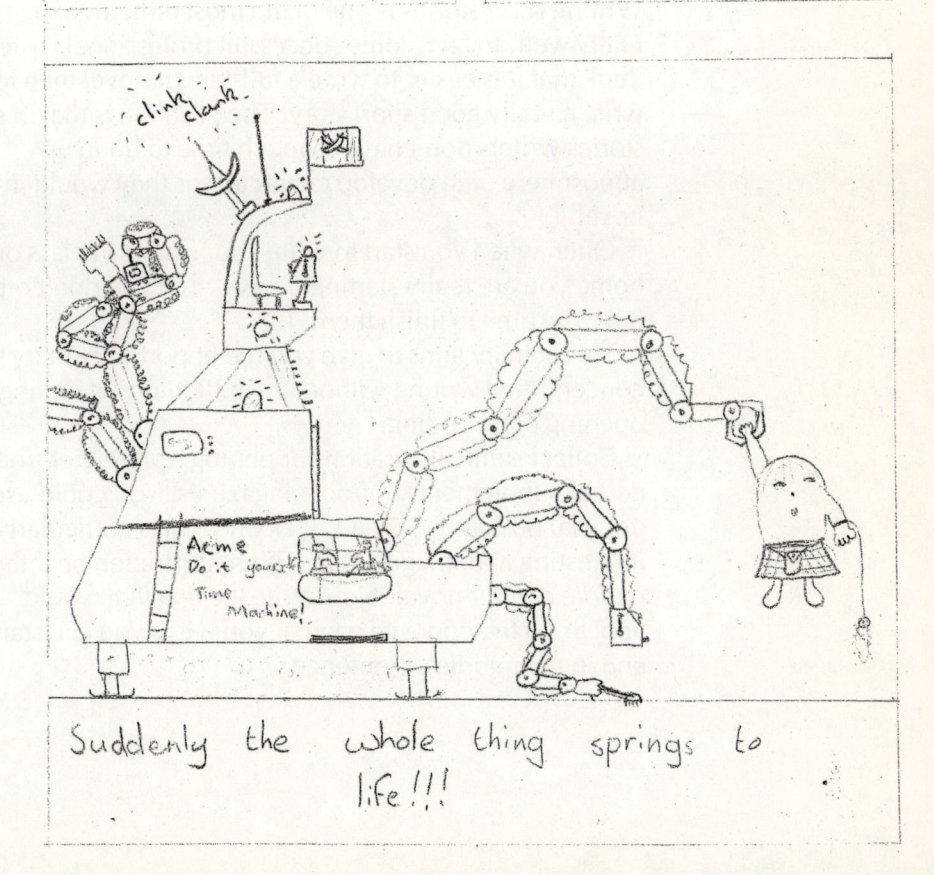

Gerald gets up and looks around.
   In one corner of the room was a great big Machine.

clink clank

Acme Do it yourself Time Machine!

Suddenly the whole thing springs to life!!!

53

Now you have a go. Plan, design and draw a cartoon strip. When you have finished, show your teacher all your plans and drafts.

What problems did you come across and how did you deal with them? Draw up a list of DOs and DON'Ts for the would-be cartoonist.

Picture book

This activity requires you to write in a way that:
- [ ] is rich in detail
- [ ] makes the reader want to read on
- [ ] is relevant to illustrations

Writing short stories is one of the most difficult things to do really well. In fact, some successful professional writers think that it is easier to write a full-length novel than to write a really good short story! The problem is that in short stories writers don't have as much time to build up atmosphere or to develop characters as they would in a novel.

Often when you start to write your stories in class or at home you are really starting novels – but you don't often have the time to finish them.

This activity aims to give you the opportunity to try some concentrated writing without the difficulties of finding an opening or an ending.

Collect some illustrations or photographs either from colour supplements or from magazines. You could use unusual postcards instead. Pick one that is particularly interesting and imagine that it is an illustration near the *middle* of your novel. Now write the text that would appear on the opposite page. If you wish, you can start and end in the middle of sentences.

3 Writing to get things done

Much of the writing you will need to do after leaving school aims to get things done. You may have to direct, persuade or correct your reader, or to explain how to go about things. This is a kind of writing in which plans, rough work and drafts are especially important.

Probably the easiest way to find out whether you are successful in this sort of writing is to see whether the reader has done what you wanted. Equally, it is easy to improve work if your reader tells you where the writing is unclear.

In this chapter you will need to bear in mind the needs of your reader, and to explain things clearly and patiently.

Holiday brochure

This activity requires you to produce writing that is:
- informative
- persuasive
- attractive and pleasing

Travel companies produce attractive catalogues or brochures describing the holidays they are trying to sell. They want to give their customers plenty of information and a pleasing impression of the holiday.

The writers of these brochures have to choose their language carefully to suit the people they are writing for. In particular, they have to consider who they expect to go on each holiday: after all, a resort which is very appealing to the 18–30 age group might not suit a family, or elderly people looking for a restful break.

The next three pages show some examples.

San Antonio

IBIZA

The biggest and busiest resort on Ibiza – one of the most lively and effervescent holiday centres in the Med. San Antonio has two faces – one for day and another for night. By day it's time for the beach, for water-skiing, sailing and windsurfing. Quite frankly, the beach at San An isn't the best in the world, but we'll do what the locals do – hop on one of the inexpensive boats to the nearby beaches of Cala Tarida or Cala Bassa – they use boats just like we use buses!

Then, as the sun sets, lights flicker on, and the West End begins to bubble. It's a warren of narrow streets spilling over with sound, colour and marvellous aromas. Pavement cafés abound. Imagine an anthill with neon lights – that's San An. If you want to treat yourself, try the shoulder of lamb at the 'Bon Proffit' restaurant – surprisingly inexpensive!

The Freestyle units are within easy reach of San Antonio. But also close to the restaurants, bars and waterchute of the southern section of San An's Bay, for those who want to escape the West End's bustle.

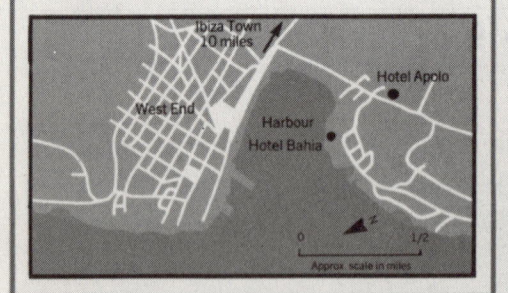

HOTEL BAHIA
1 2 3 4

Twenty minutes walk from San Antonio's night time heart, the West End, the Bahia is situated right on the sea front. Well furnished and comfortable, the hotel boasts several communal facilities including a pool table and a very comfortably furnished lounge.

Many of the bedrooms have great views over the bay that gives the hotel its name. Also overlooking the bay there's a sun terrace and an oval shaped pool in front of the hotel. Just beyond that is a jetty from where water taxis ferry people to San An centre and some of the best beaches on the island. If you prefer not to go into San Antonio every night, the Bahia is splendidly placed to take advantage of the local nightlife. Next door but one is the Jade, Ibiza's popular Chinese restaurant, close by is the Taj Mahal Indian restaurant, and within easy striking distance is the Fiesta Bar, the south side's most popular music and meeting place.

Prices shown are per person for bed and breakfast in a room with two or three beds with bath and wc. Some 4 bedded rooms are available.
Supplements (per person per night): balcony 50p, single room with shower and wc £2.50.

Fuengirola Costa del Sol

Fuengirola is a bustling resort with an enormous amount of charm, located midway between Torremolinos and Marbella. As well as being a holiday centre, Fuengirola is the second home for many Spaniards, who have beautiful villas dotted around the area. The resort's glorious beach is flanked by a long, flat promenade where you'll find lots of pavement cafés and bars. There are masses of shops in the resort and plenty of nightlife, including clubs, bars and restaurants, some with local musicians to entertain you as you dine out in style. Apart from our exciting excursions, you can also go sightseeing under your own steam as there are frequent bus services to Marbella and Torremolinos and a train operates every half hour throughout the day between Malaga and Fuengirola. Your coach transfer from Malaga airport takes about 40 minutes.

The El Puerto Sol

Fuengirola

YOUNG HEART

EXTRAS INCLUDED!

★ Free sightseeing excursion ★ Half-price excursion to Marbella and Puerto Banus ★ Young at Heart welcome party plus 'get to know the area' walk ★ Welcome tea and biscuits ★ Bingo twice a week, board games ★ Whist ★ Quizzes, competitions and fancy dress ★ Dancing twice a week ★ Newspaper/magazine club ★ Weekly cookery demonstration ★ Language classes ★ Young at Heart I.D.C. Discount Card

Also included Sol Savers ★ Daytime activities programme including video films, cooking classes and darts ★ Evening entertainments programme including games, competitions and shows plus dancing to records or band most nights ★ Activities programme for 'older' holiday-makers ★ Special present for honeymooners, birthdays, silver or gold anniversaries ★ Daily Happy Hour ★ Reduced green fees at nearby golf course

Special Extras on Certain Departures ★ Full Board at Half Board prices ★ No single room supplement And lots more besides!!! For details see page 47

HOTEL EL PUERTO SOL ттт

Welcoming you with a friendly and informal atmosphere, this outstanding modern hotel is part of the Sol group - noted for their high standards of comfort, service and entertainment. It is attractively furnished throughout with a nautical theme, and a layout reflecting its distinctive twin-tower design. Young at Heart guests often remark on the good food here.

Location Very well placed on the Paseo Maritimo, the attractive promenade (flat ground all the way) which extends for some 2 miles along the seafront. Just a couple of minutes' walk along and across the road is the sandy beach, and there's a fishing port close by too. This hotel is very central with the shops, cafés, snack bars and night-spots of the main town centre about 5 minutes away. It is about 10 minutes' walk to the bus stop; another few minutes bring you to the station for the local Fuengirola-Torremolinos-Malaga railway.

Features On the ground floor, the spacious reception foyer leads to an open plan lounge overlooking the promenade where you can sit and chat and just off it is the El Boliche bar. There is also a small dance floor where there is dancing most nights. On the first floor - by lift, or up the circular staircase - is the light and airy restaurant (self-service buffet for all meals). Over the Christmas period enjoy the hotel's Christmas and New Year Gala meals. Next to it is another comfortable lounge, a games room and a card room. There is also a television room. From this level, you can step out onto the sun-terrace overlooking the port. For an even finer view, walk up to the rooftop terrace surrounding the circular swimming pool. Table-tennis is also available and you can play tennis at the nearby Hotel Las Palmeras (equipment for hire) which also has the bonus of a bowls green situated next door. Central heating in all rooms.

Our Opinion It couldn't be better located - right in the heart of Fuengirola. There are several stairways, but they are the only possible drawback to this lively holiday hotel.

Prices shown are per person for half board in a room with two or three beds, with private bath, wc and balcony. Supplement (per person per night): full board £1.85.

Reduction (per night): for 3rd adult only in room £1.55

Official Rating: ***; Hotel Bedrooms: 318; Lifts: 3 in each tower
Telephone No: 010 34 52 470100

THEME WEEKS

Special Golf Theme Week holiday available from April 10th, see page 5 for details.

Cookery demonstration

LONGSTAY

42 nights departing 4 Dec price **£499**

For room and meal details and any supplements see hotel description.

Flights and supplements (see pp 44 & 45) Gatwick (3202) £0, Luton (3208) £3, Birmingham (3213) £9, Manchester (3220) £13, Newcastle (3226) £22, Glasgow (3229) £29.

For 56 night holidays throughout the season see the price panel

Examples of holiday brochures

GREECE MIXED NEW AND OLD, DAYS BRONZED, NIGHTS GOLD

RHODES
FROM £171

Legend has it that Rhodes was once the home of the Sun God Helios — whether it's true or not isn't really important, but we do know that Rhodes has the best sunshine record in the Greek Islands and that has to be good for sunseekers everywhere!
Rhodes really is a delightful place, filled with pine forests, olive groves, beautiful beaches and great holiday resorts with real character and charm. If you plan to be in Rhodes during July to September take time to visit the Valley of Butterflies (no nets please!) in Petaloudes where you'll see millions of colourful butterflies — it's pretty spectacular! Another good excursion is to the village of Lindos with its narrow streets and quaint buildings at the foot of the Acropolis.
All the resorts in Rhodes have their own attractions, with open air cafes, beach restaurants and bars, seafood tavernas and lively local nightspots. Shopping here is a pleasure with low duty prices on most goods and don't forget to haggle with the traders in the Turkish Bazaar and Mandraki Market — they enjoy it almost as much as you do. You'll find Rhodes perfect for your holiday in the sun!

RHODES TOWN

Rhodes town has an interesting contrast of old and new attractions. Behind the walls of the old city you step back in time as you stroll through narrow winding tree shaded streets, mediaeval palaces, exotic bazaars and mosques — everything a history buff could wish for! New Rhodes overlooks the beautiful harbour on one side and the long sandy beach on the other. Rhodes is reputed to be among the most sophisticated resorts in Greece with an exciting, varied nightlife and more bars, clubs and restaurants than you could sample in a month of Sundays. The atmosphere is electric so it's easy to understand why Rhodes is so popular — especially with young people. Come to Rhodes with Twentys, and enjoy the best of both worlds — you won't regret it!

NIGHT
Greek Night ▷ Night Cruise with BBQ ▷ Ixia Disco Trip ▷ Faliraki by night ▷ Fancy Dress Party ▷ Bazouki Night ▷ Butterflies Traditional Greek Taverna ▷ Mandy's Chinese Restaurant ▷ Kontiki Floating Restaurant in Mandraki Harbour ▷ Poseidon

& DAY
East Coast Cruise ▷ Lindos by day ▷ Windsurfing ▷ Waterskiing ▷ Sailing ▷ Scuba Diving ▷ Ski-Biking ▷ Waterslides

Design and write a page for a holiday brochure about a resort you have visited, or one that you have made up. You might include ideas from this list:
- ☐ a description of the resort and beaches
- ☐ information about the hotel or accommodation
- ☐ details of sport and leisure facilities
- ☐ information about special amenities (such as for children)
- ☐ a guide to the local nightlife
- ☐ lists of tourist attractions
- ☐ maps
- ☐ photographs of people having a good time

The confidential notebook

Travel agents sometimes keep a confidential record of what their customers said about a holiday when they came back, especially if it did not live up to their expectations. You might like to write an entry in this confidential record about your resort.

Theme park

This activity asks you:
- ☐ to exercise your imagination
- ☐ to write persuasively and clearly for other people
- ☐ to present work in an appropriate and attractive way

Design a park for holidaymakers and day visitors, based on a theme such as water sports, fantasy or technology.
- Draw a *map* of the theme park.
- Design a *poster* advertising it to the public.
- Prepare a *brochure* to attract potential customers.
- Design a *car-sticker* (for adults) and a *badge* (for children) to take home as souvenirs.
- Record a *radio advertisement* for a 20-second commercial break.
- Draw up a *notice* announcing the day's organised activities.

Writing to get things done

Promoting music

This activity encourages you to use language which is:
- ☐ suitable to the product
- ☐ appealing to the customer
- ☐ fair and informative, as well as persuasive

You are Director of Promotions in a small, newly-established recording company, RGS Records. You have recently signed a highly talented new band who write their own material. You now want to promote them in as many ways as possible. In addition, they have enough songs already written to make up their first album and their manager wants this to come out as soon as possible.

Your small promotions team decides to tackle the challenge in a number of ways:
- publicity *hand-outs* on the group, for the music papers and for the teenage magazines
- a *promotion pack*, which could include sleeve notes of the album and lyrics
- a *pull-out sheet* with the lyrics of the songs on the album
- radio and TV *interviews* for members of the group
- favourable *reviews* of their last couple of releases
- part of the *storyboard* of their video
- an *account* of their background and rise to fame (from a colour supplement)
- car *stickers*, *T-shirts* and *badges*

Words only

This activity encourages you:
- ☐ to be exact
- ☐ to write in a logical order
- ☐ to give clear descriptions

If we cannot give instructions in person, or if no example is available, we must rely on the power of words to communicate what is to be done. This activity asks you to

Words only

prepare instructions in writing, without the aid of diagrams.

The tennis court

Fred, whose job it is to mark out the tennis courts at the local park, has broken his leg while on holiday in Majorca. His assistant, Bill, has to do the job instead. But Bill is no expert: he has no idea how to lay out the court.

Here is a diagram of a tennis court. Using words only, tell Bill how to set about it.

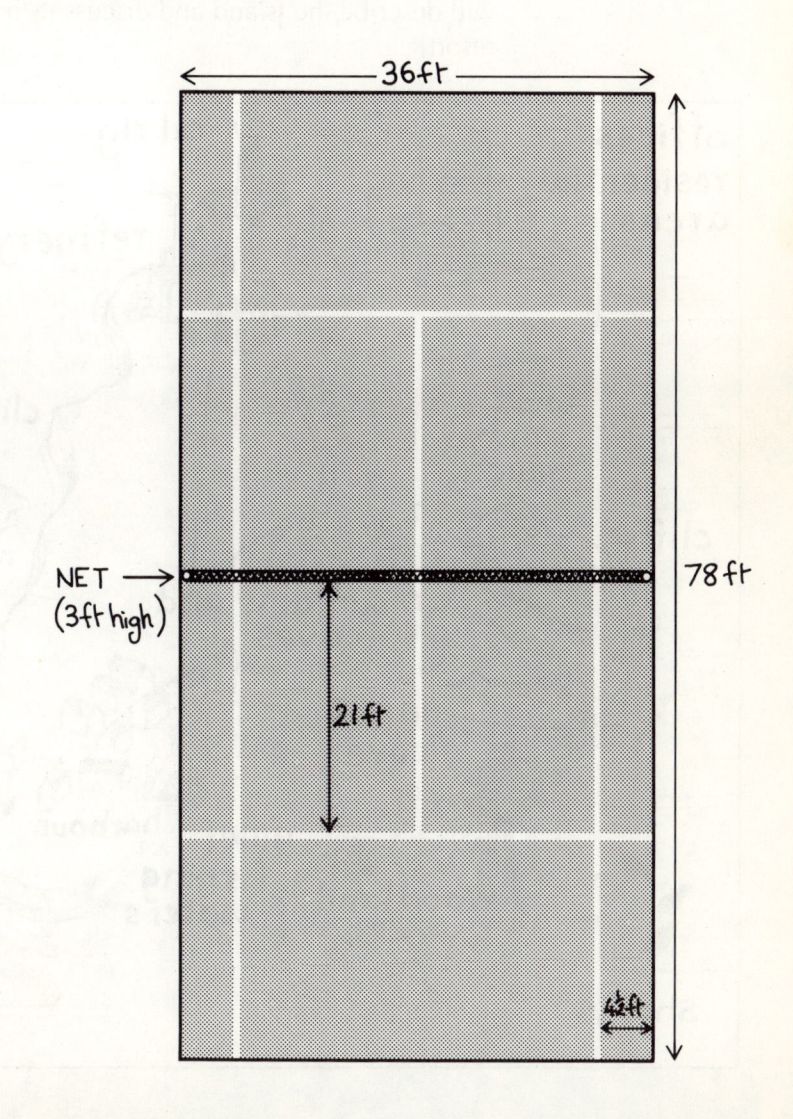

Writing to get things done

The island

Gina is employed by a large travel company to seek out new holiday resorts. She is due to make a report at an important meeting about the island of Torredorm in the Mediterranean. Unfortunately Gina is at this moment stranded at Luton Airport, and you have to make the report instead. All you have is this sketch which Gina has left on her desk.

You do not have time to prepare visual aids for the meeting. Use the sketch to write a verbal report which will describe the island and discuss its potential as a resort.

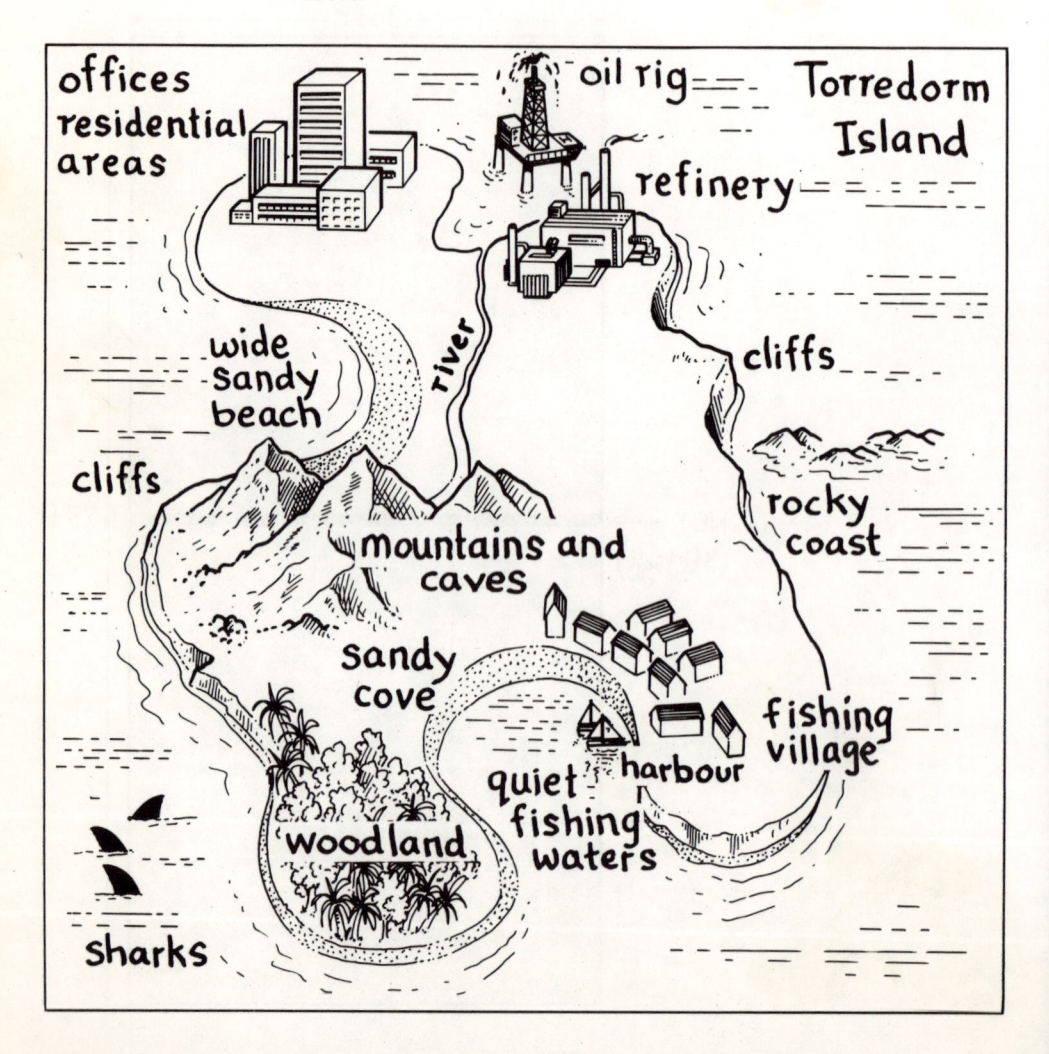

Words only

The mobile

Using the diagram below, explain in words, as if to a parent, how to put together this simple mobile. The items are provided ready-made but not assembled.

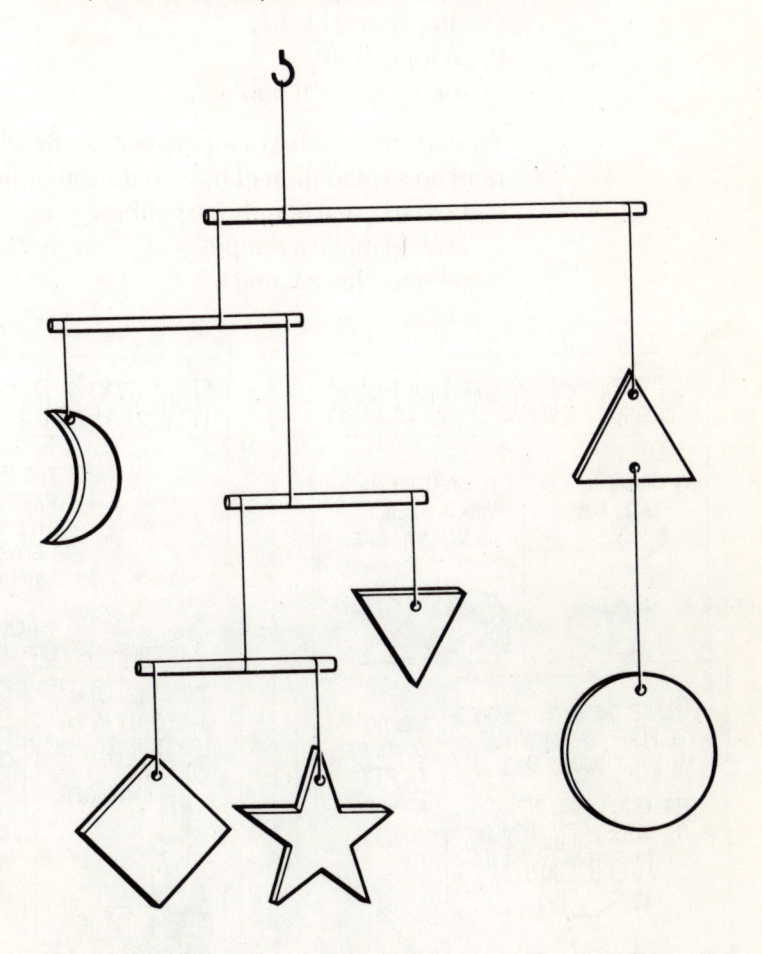

Afterwards, read aloud your instructions to each other and discuss which ones you find clear and easy to follow. Discuss the following points:
- When are diagrams helpful?
- When is it not possible to use diagrams?
- When is it not desirable to use diagrams?
- What tips would you give someone writing descriptions or instructions without the benefit of diagrams?

63

Writing to get things done

Telling how

This is an exercise in writing:
- ☐ simply and clearly
- ☐ in logical steps
- ☐ for the general public

To start, make a list of all the occasions when you might read an explanation of how to do something – for example,
> how to use a telephone callbox
> how to make a recipe
> how to play a game

How to perform a magic trick

What makes a good explanation?
   Choose two of the easier items on your list. Explain – as if to someone who is sensible but inexperienced – how to

64

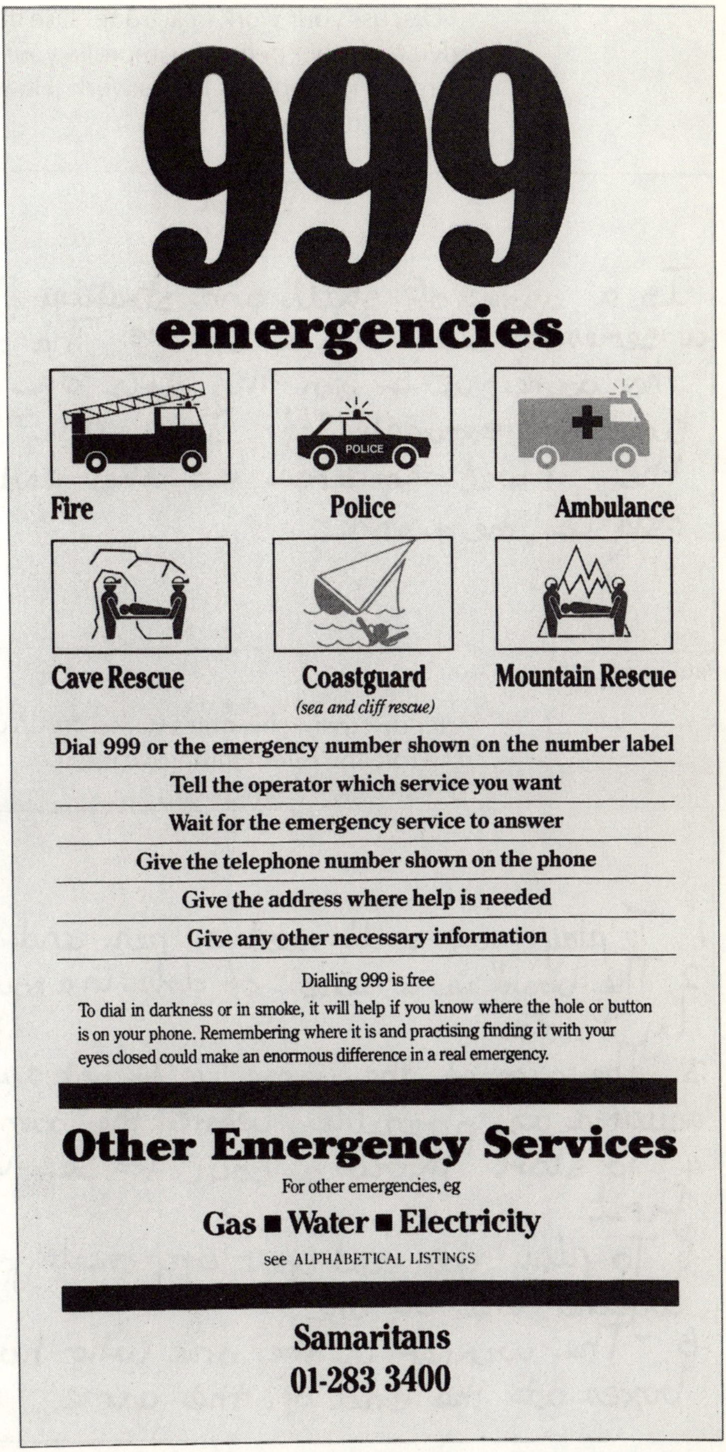

Telling how

999
emergencies

Fire **Police** **Ambulance**

Cave Rescue **Coastguard** **Mountain Rescue**
(sea and cliff rescue)

Dial 999 or the emergency number shown on the number label

Tell the operator which service you want

Wait for the emergency service to answer

Give the telephone number shown on the phone

Give the address where help is needed

Give any other necessary information

Dialling 999 is free

To dial in darkness or in smoke, it will help if you know where the hole or button is on your phone. Remembering where it is and practising finding it with your eyes closed could make an enormous difference in a real emergency.

Other Emergency Services

For other emergencies, eg

Gas ■ Water ■ Electricity

see ALPHABETICAL LISTINGS

Samaritans
01-283 3400

How to make a 999 emergency call

Writing to get things done

go about doing each of the two things.

Discuss your work in a group. Use the comments and advice of other people to improve your explanations. Here, for example, is Paul's work. He was writing the rules to the game *Boxes*.

> **Boxes**
>
> Is a game of skill and strategy. There are a series of dots in a square. The object of the game is to pen the dots one go at a time, for example ∴ The one with the most squares at the end of the day is the winner.

Paul's first draft

After discussing his notes with a group of friends he re-wrote the rules to improve them.

> 1. To play you will need a pen and paper.
> 2. The board is a series of dots in a square 8 dots by 8 dots.
> 3. The aim of the game is to get as many squares as possible before the game is over.
> 4. To start throw a coin to see who goes first.
> 5. To play you and your opponent join the dots together one by one.
> 6. The winner is the one who has the most boxes at the end of the game.

Telling how

He tried out his rules on some other students who did not know the game. Realising that there was something missing, he added in the following note:

> 5. To play. First of all you throw a coin to see who is going to start the game. Then you join the dots in turn. When you get a box you get a free go. When you get a box you put your initials in it.

> **Boxes**
>
> 1. Boxes is a game of skill and strategy for two players.
> 2. To play you will need a pen and paper.
> 3. The board is a series of dots in a square 8 dots by 8 dots.
> 4. The aim of the game is to get as many squares as possible.
> 5. To start throw a coin to see who goes first.
> 6. To play. First of all throw a coin to see who is going to start the game. Then you join the dots in turn. When you get a box you get a free go. When you get a box you put your initials in it.
> 7. The winner is the one with the most boxes at the end of it.

Paul's final version

67

4 Telling tales

We hear stories and we tell stories from an early age. Stories can entertain, warn or explain things to us. Underneath a simple-sounding tale there is often deep meaning.

In this chapter we present some old story-telling ideas such as fables and fairy stories, and also some new ones such as the mini-saga and the pocket-story. We suspect that the appeal of stories is the same for everyone, and only the fashion changes.

Oral literature

In this activity, we hope to make you aware of:
- [ ] the literature you have inherited
- [ ] your own amazing memory
- [ ] your natural appetite for stories and poems

All your life you have been listening to stories and songs and poems – but you have heard them rather than read them. You have memorised scores of *poems*:
- [ ] pop songs
- [ ] nursery rhymes
- [ ] hymns
- [ ] lullabies
- [ ] limericks
- [ ] songs that go with games
- [ ] Christmas carols   (such as skipping songs)

Can you think of others?

You have also memorised many *stories*:
- [ ] fairy tales   [ ] anecdotes   [ ] jokes

Can you think of others?

You also know many *sayings*:
- [ ] jingles   [ ] proverbs   [ ] prayers

Can you think of others?

We call all of this *oral literature* – stories, poems, songs and sayings that are passed on by word of mouth.

Collect examples of oral literature – on a tape recorder, if possible. You might like to choose a theme, such as:
- lullabies
- songs that go with games
- your own favourites

Older people will remember the songs and stories they learnt as children, and though you may recognise them, the words will probably have changed over the years. Older people are a good source of material when you are collecting examples of oral literature.

Mini-sagas

This activity will encourage you to:
- choose your words with care
- sort out the essential from the inessential
- improve your work by drafting

A *mini-saga* is a short story, exactly 50 words long – not a word more, not a word less. It must be a story that says something worthwhile – something more than just an anecdote or a description. You can choose a title too, but it must be no more than 15 words long.

The next three pages show some examples.

Telling tales

UPSIDE DOWN IN A FIRE DRILL

It was Blogend school,
(My school fire drill).
Mr. Fenwick (headmaster)
found me upside down in a
rubbish bin, waving my feet
like a helicopter, about to
take off.
'What are you doing?' asked
Mr. Fenwick.
'Panicking, sir!' I answered
He suddenly turned as red
as a beetroot.
'Trust you!'

ANDREW WATTS
Devizes   Age 10

THE POSTCARD

Friendless, he despatched
a letter to the twelfth
century. Illuminated scrolls
arrived by return post.
Jottings to Tutankhamun
secured
hieroglyphs on papyrus;
Hannibal sent
a campaign report.
But when he addressed the
future, hoping for cassettes
crammed with wonders, a
postcard drifted back with
scorched edges. It glowed
all night.

GUY CARTER
London W1

THE INNER MAN

Their marriage was
a perfect union of trust
and understanding. They
shared everything – except
his desk drawer, which,
through the years, remained
locked.
One day, curiosity
overcame her. Prised open,
there was – nothing.
'But why?' she asked,
confused and ashamed.
'I needed a space of my
own', he replied sadly.

CHRISTINE M. BANKS

THE DEATH TOUCH

When a daughter went
away to college, she reluctantly
left her plants and her
goldfish in her mother's care.
Once the daughter telephoned
and her mother confessed
that the plants and
the goldfish had died.
There was a prolonged silence.
Finally, in a small voice,
the daughter asked,
'How's Dad?'

DAWN HUNT
Stafford

Telling tales

A TRIP TO THE BIG WET ONE

Forced from the car,
I dread the big wet one.
Approaching her door, my mind
is frozen with dread. The
door opens. A flesh mountain
in an oversize dress towers
before me. I am lifted off
my feet and face the rubbery
lips. It comes ... the
big wet one ... smack!

MATTHEW EMBER
Wembley Park   Age 10

It takes time to write a mini-saga. Be prepared to cut and change words in order to get the best from your 50-word allowance. You will probably need to write several drafts.

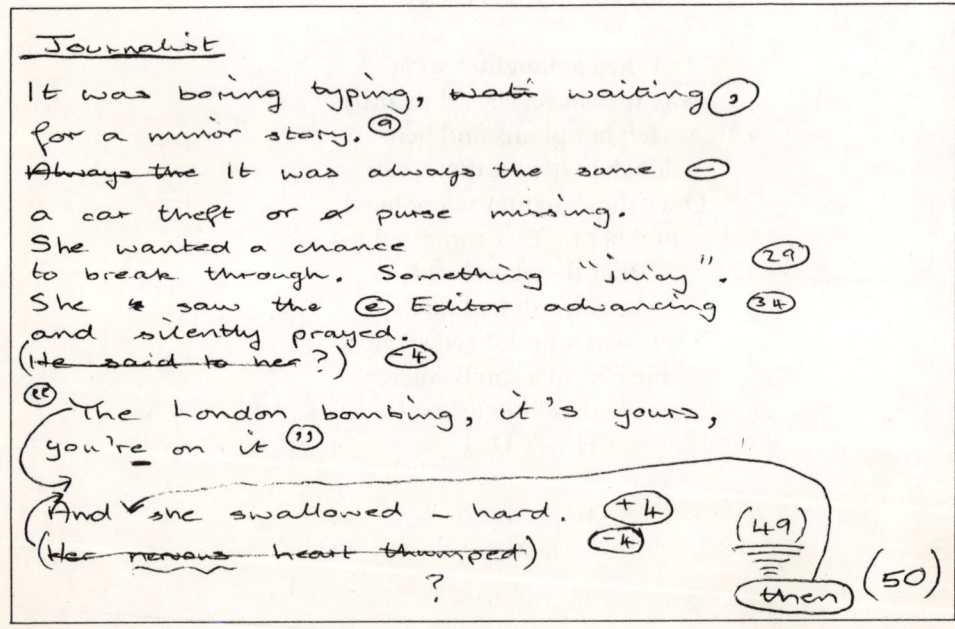

> <u>Journalist</u>
>
> It was boring typing, ~~wati~~ waiting
> for a minor story.
> ~~Always the~~ It was always the same
> a car theft or a purse missing.
> She wanted a chance
> to break through. Something "juicy".
> She ~~*~~ saw the Editor advancing
> and silently prayed.
> (~~He said to her?~~)
> "The London bombing, it's yours,
> you're on it"
> (And she swallowed — hard.)
> (~~Her nervous heart thumped~~)
>   ?
>   (49)
>   then (50)

Melanie's draft

Mini-sagas

> Journalist
>
> It was boring typing, waiting
> for a minor story.
> It was always the same —
> a car theft or purse missing.
> She wanted a chance
> to break through. Something "juicy".
> She saw the editor advancing,
> and silently prayed.
> "The London bombing, it's yours,
> you're on it."
> And then she swallowed — hard.

Melanie's final version

> TITLE??
>
> The nights are cold, 4
> the days are burning. 8
> The sun grows brighter. 12
> Panic(ed) ants dance on the 17
> face of the Earth. Decisions are made. 24
> The days are burning O 28
> The planet launches insignificant 32
> silver slivers, bearing humanit(ies) fruits(:) 37
> Tiny ants, sitting in their ships, 43
> watching the sun growing, 47
> ~~burning~~ consuming their(?) world. 50

Peter's draft

Telling tales

> **Dancing in a Refuge**
>
> The nights are cold,
> the days are burning.
> The sun grows brighter.
> Panicked ants dance on the
> face of the Earth. Decisions are made.
>   The days are burning.
>   The planet launches insignificant
>   silver slivers, bearing humanity's fruits:
>   Tiny ants, sitting in their ships
>   watch the sun grow,
>   consuming the world.

Peter's final version

Angeline's mini-saga (below) developed after many changes to her first draft (opposite).

> **THE MARRIAGE**
>
> She put up with his bad words,
>   his violence and his
>   resounding curse
> for twenty years and thirty days.
> And when the marriage was
>   lying black, cold and dead,
>   and her hopeless heart about to break,
>   he smiled.
> With a tear in her eye, all she heard
>   was the crack.

Angeline's final version

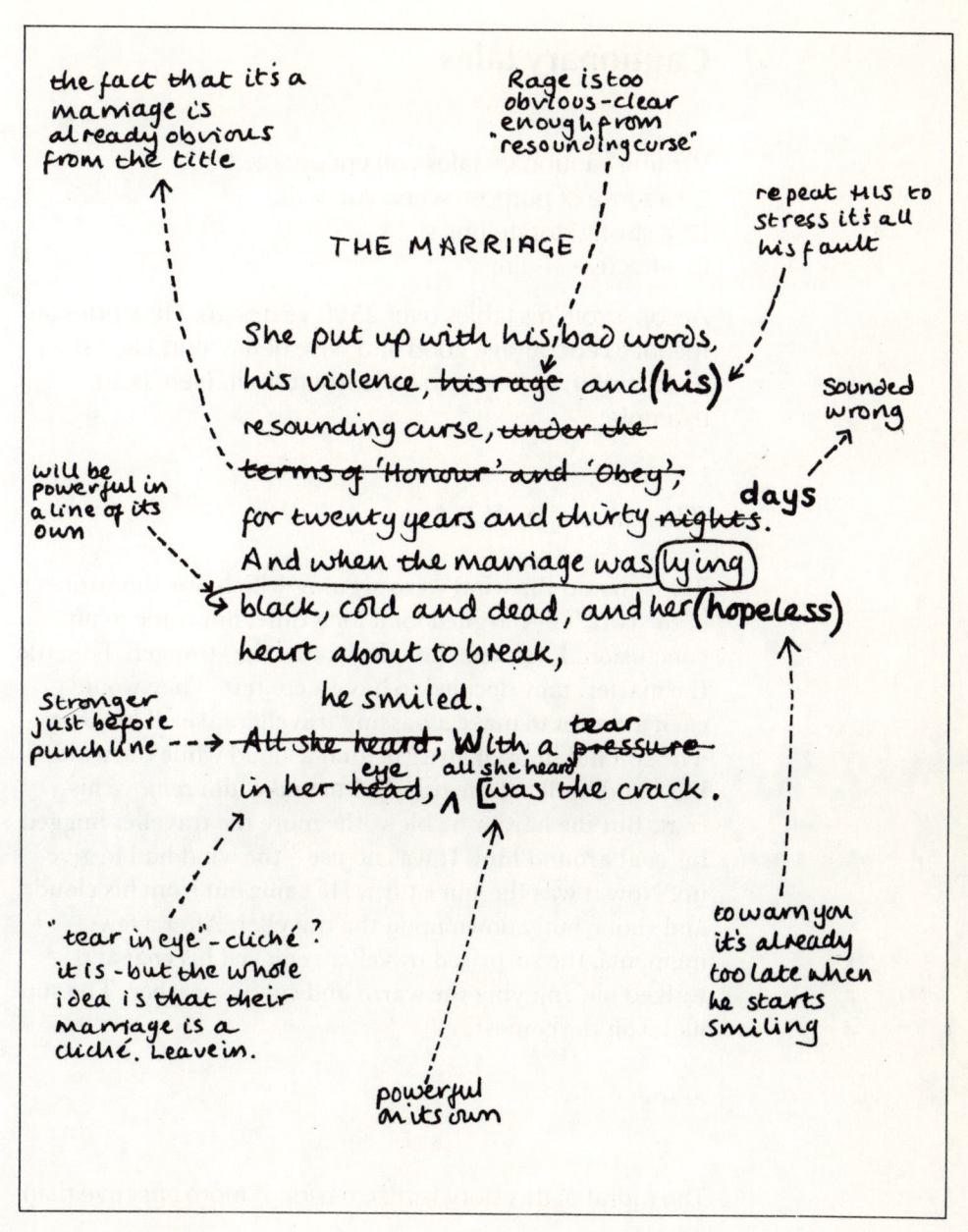

Mini-sagas

THE MARRIAGE

(Angeline's draft, with handwritten annotations:)

She put up with his bad words, his violence, ~~his rage~~ and (his) resounding curse, ~~under the terms of 'Honour' and 'Obey',~~ for twenty years and thirty ~~nights~~ days. And when the marriage was lying black, cold and dead, and her (hopeless) heart about to break, he smiled. ~~All she heard,~~ With a tear in her ~~head~~ eye, all she heard ~~pressure~~ [was the crack.

Annotations:
- the fact that it's a marriage is already obvious from the title
- Rage is too obvious – clear enough from "resounding curse"
- repeat HIS to stress it's all his fault
- Sounded wrong
- will be powerful in a line of its own
- to warn you it's already too late when he starts smiling
- Stronger just before punch line
- "tear in eye" – cliché? it is – but the whole idea is that their marriage is a cliché. Leave in.
- powerful on its own

Angeline's draft

Now you try writing a mini-saga. Remember:
- ☐ 50 words exactly
- ☐ title of no more than 15 words
- ☐ the mini-saga must be a complete story

Cautionary tales

Writing cautionary tales will encourage:
- a sense of purpose when you write
- a strong storytelling style
- effective endings

Aesop wrote his tables over 2500 years ago. His stories are meant to encourage good and wise behaviour. Each story has a *moral*, or lesson to be learnt from it. Here is an example:

The Sun and the Wind

The sun and the wind were arguing which was the stronger of the two. They argued for a long time, but came to no conclusion. Each one thought he was the stronger. To settle the matter, they decided to have a contest. They would each attempt to make a passing traveller take off his coat. The sun hid himself away behind a cloud while the wind blew and buffeted the traveller to make him remove his coat. But the harder he blew, the more the traveller hugged his coat around him. It was no use – the wind had to give up. Now it was the sun's turn. He came out from his cloud and shone hotly down upon the traveller. After a few moments, the surprised traveller removed his coat and walked on, enjoying the warm and sunny weather. The sun had won the contest.

AESOP

The moral of this story is: *Persuasion is more effective than force.*

Here is another story. Can you work out the moral?

The Arrow

One day an eagle was flying in the mountains. A hunter saw the bird and quickly prepared his bow and arrow to shoot it down. The poor bird was struck through the heart by the arrow, and in his dying moments as he fell to earth, he recognised the feathers in the arrow as his own.

AESOP

What is the moral of this story? Write down your answer. Compare your answer with other people's answers. Discuss which is the best.

Here are two further stories to discuss:

Bird Woman

Once there was a child who sprouted wings. They sprang from her shoulder blades, and at first they were vestigial. But they grew rapidly, and in no time at all she had a sizeable wing span. The neighbours were horrified. 'You must have them cut,' they said to her parents. 'Why?' said her parents. 'Well, it's obvious,' said the neighbours. 'No,' said the parents, and this seemed so final that the neighbours left. But a few weeks later the neighbours were back. 'If you won't have them cut, at least have them clipped.' 'Why?' said the parents. 'Well, at least it shows that you're doing something.' 'No,' said the parents, and the neighbours left. Then for the third time the neighbours appeared. 'On at least two occasions you have sent us away,' they informed the parents, 'but think of that child. What are you doing to the poor little thing?' 'We are teaching her to fly,' said the parents quietly.

SUNITI NAMJOSHI

Telling tales

The Doll

Two little girls are making a doll. It's a male doll. It's made out of sticks. Perched on the sticks is a round stone. That is its head. The doll is fragile. A boy comes along. He stares at the doll. The little girls tell him that the name of the doll is Brittle Boy. The boy gets mad. He smashes the doll. The two little girls get very angry. They would like very much to smash the boy. But they say to themselves that the boy is fragile. They pick up the sticks, and start over.

SUNITI NAMJOSHI

Can you think of everyday situations to which these stories apply?

Now write a tale to warn children of the perils of *one* of these:
- ☐ telling tales
- ☐ boasting
- ☐ being cheeky
- ☐ cheating
- ☐ staying out late

Alternatively, choose a famous proverb – such as
- ☐ Too many cooks spoil the broth
- ☐ Waste not, want not
- ☐ More haste, less speed

– and write a story to illustrate it.

Pocket stories

Pocket stories demand:
- ☐ careful planning
- ☐ logic
- ☐ a sense of genre

Some types of story, or *genres*, are very popular. Here are some examples:

Pocket stories

> spy stories
> detective stories
> love stories
>
> Can you think of any other types?

We enjoy these stories when we read them in books, or watch them on television or at the cinema or theatre.
  Choose one type of story to discuss in detail.
- Start by thinking of examples of the genre. Note them on a diagram, like this:

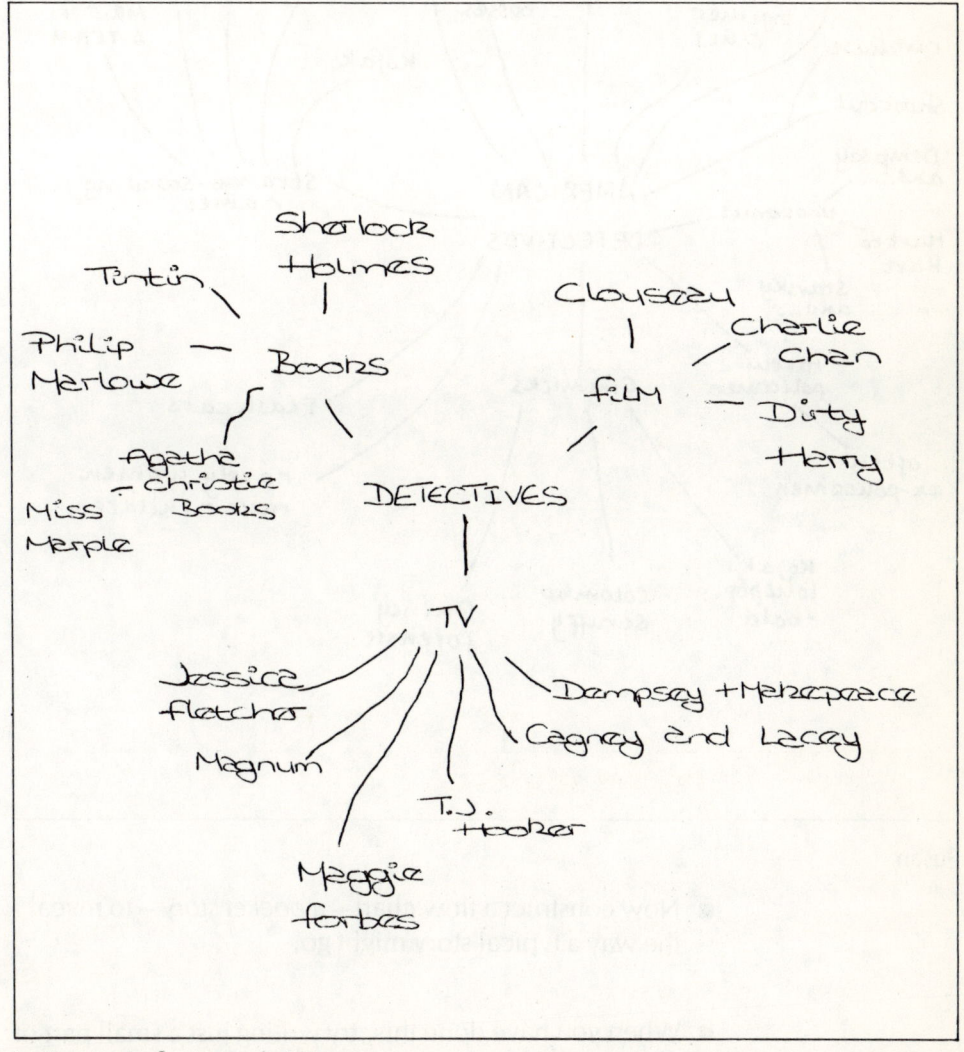

(Diagram of DETECTIVES with branches:)

- Books: Tintin, Sherlock Holmes, Philip Marlowe, Agatha Christie Books, Miss Marple
- Film: Clouseau, Charlie Chan, Dirty Harry
- TV: Jessica Fletcher, Magnum, T.J. Hooker, Maggie Forbes, Dempsey + Makepeace, Cagney and Lacey

Justin, Andrew, Anna and Sharon

Telling tales

- What are the typical ingredients for your type of story? Keep a note of your ideas, like this:

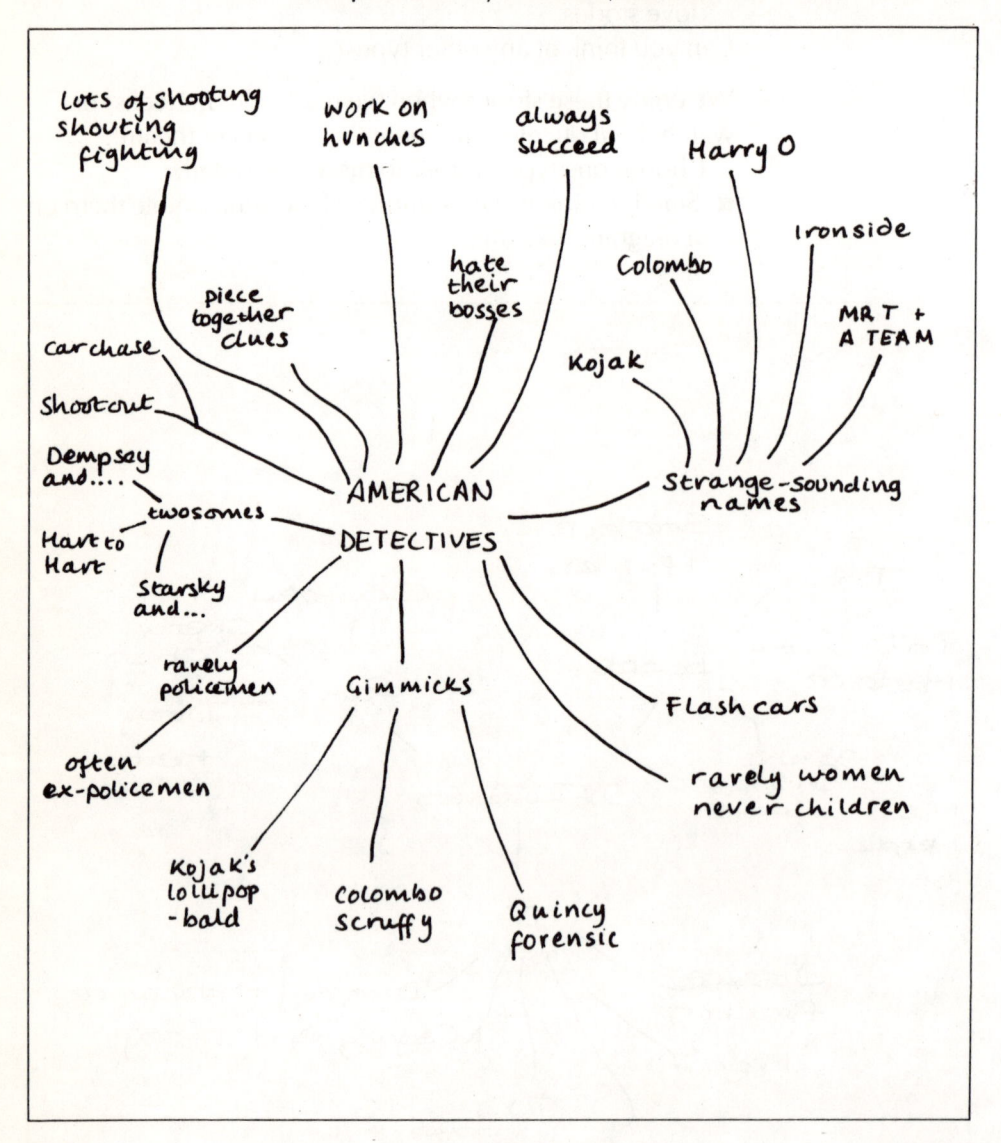

Central topic: **AMERICAN DETECTIVES**

- Lots of shooting, shouting, fighting
- work on hunches
- always succeed
- Harry O
- Ironside
- piece together clues
- hate their bosses
- Colombo
- MR T + A TEAM
- car chase
- Shootout
- Kojak
- Dempsey and....
- twosomes
- Strange-sounding names
- Hart to Hart
- Starsky and...
- rarely policemen
- Gimmicks
- Flash cars
- often ex-policemen
- rarely women never children
- Kojak's lollipop - bald
- Colombo scruffy
- Quincy forensic

Susan

- Now construct a flow chart – a *pocket story* – to reveal the way a typical story might go.

- When you have done this, try writing just a small part of the story, such as the opening, the climax or the ending.

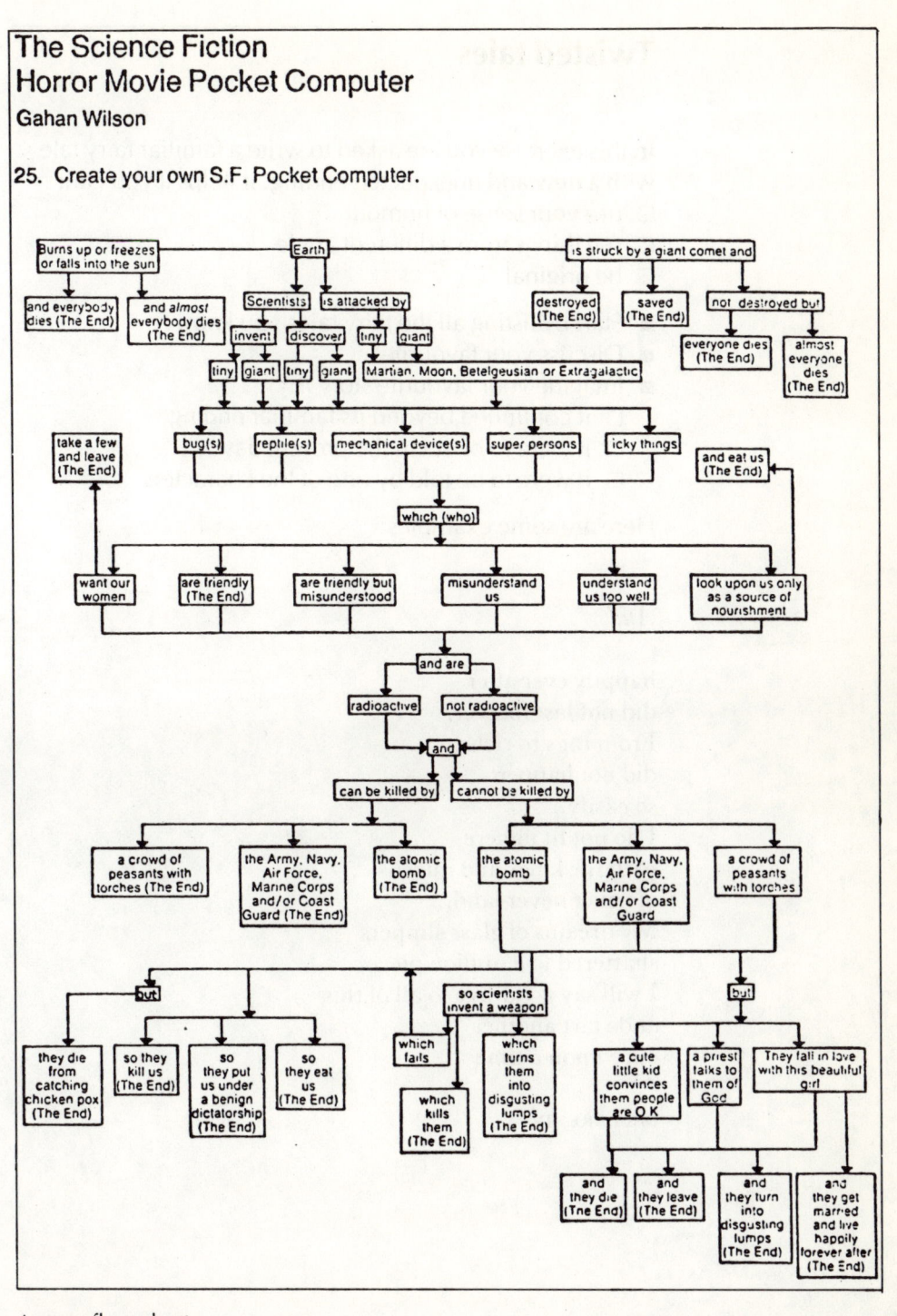

The Science Fiction Horror Movie Pocket Computer

Gahan Wilson

25. Create your own S.F. Pocket Computer.

A story flow chart

```
                    Earth
        ┌─────────────┼──────────────────────────┐
Burns up or freezes                    is struck by a giant comet and
or falls into the sun                   ┌──────┬──────┬──────────┐
   ┌────┴────┐                      destroyed  saved  not destroyed but
and everybody  and almost              (The End) (The End)  ┌────┴────┐
dies (The End) everybody dies                           everyone dies  almost
                                                         (The End)   everyone
   Scientists    is attacked by                                        dies
   ┌───┴────┐    ┌───┴───┐                                           (The End)
 invent  discover tiny  giant
   │        │      │      │
  tiny  giant tiny giant   Martian, Moon, Betelgeusian or Extragalactic
   └────┬───┴───┬──┴──────┬──────────────┬────────────┐
      bug(s) reptile(s) mechanical device(s) super persons  icky things
                         │                                      │
                    which (who)                            and eat us
                         │                                  (The End)
   ┌────────┬────────────┼──────────────┬──────────┐
want our  are friendly  are friendly but misunderstand understand  look upon us only
women    (The End)     misunderstood      us         us too well  as a source of
   │                                                               nourishment
take a few
and leave              and are
(The End)          ┌─────┴─────┐
              radioactive  not radioactive
                   └─────┬─────┘
                        and
                   ┌─────┴─────┐
              can be killed by  cannot be killed by
   ┌──────────┬────────┤              ├────────┬──────────┐
a crowd of  the Army, Navy,  the atomic   the atomic  the Army, Navy,  a crowd of
peasants    Air Force,      bomb          bomb        Air Force,       peasants
with torches Marine Corps  (The End)                  Marine Corps     with torches
(The End)   and/or Coast                              and/or Coast
            Guard (The End)                           Guard

   ┌──┴──┐                  so scientists                  └──┴──┐
  but                       invent a weapon                     but
   │                         ┌────┴────┐                         │
┌──┬──┬──┐                  which    which              ┌───┬───┬───┐
they  so they  so they  so  fails    turns them         a cute priest They fall in love
die   kill us  put us   they           into             little talks to with this beautiful
from  (The End) under a  eat           disgusting       kid    them of  girl
catching       benign    us            lumps           convinces God
chicken pox    dictatorship (The End) (The End)        them people
(The End)     (The End)                                are O.K.
                         which
                         kills
                         them
                         (The End)
                                           ┌────┬────┬────┐
                                          and  and  and  and
                                          they they they they
                                          die  leave turn  get
                                        (The End)(The End) into married
                                                     disgusting and live
                                                     lumps      happily
                                                     (The End)  forever after
                                                                (The End)
```

81

Telling tales

Twisted tales

In this exercise you are asked to write a familiar fairy tale with a new and unexpected ending. It helps if you can:
- ☐ use your sense of humour
- ☐ see things from a different angle
- ☐ be original

- ■ Start by listing all the fairy tales you know.
- ■ Discuss your favourites.
- ■ Imagine your favourite story *if*:
  - ☐ it continued beyond its familiar ending
  - ☐ it were to be set in the present day
  - ☐ it were to be told by one of the characters

Here are some examples:

And

happily ever after
did not last forever.
From rags to riches
did not happen
so easily.
I do not fit in here
with the kings and queens
of never never land.
My dreams of glass slippers
shattered to a million pieces
I will say good-bye to all of this
and start another
once upon a time

DEBI BRENIN

Snow White's Prince

Oh, woe is me.
Why did I ever choose
that route through the forest?
Hundreds of ways but I had to choose
the route that destined me
to a life with Snow White.
Everyone thinks we lived happily
ever after,
a handsome young prince and a beautiful maiden,
a match made in heaven.
I wish the world knew the true story.
Nobody ever told me
about Snow White's large family
which visits, constantly.
Nobody told me how attached she was
to the seven dwarfs
that they would move in with us.
Nobody told me that the witch had a sister
who would seek revenge.
I am beginning to think that with my kiss
that gave Snow White life
I ended mine.

BILLY FRISCHLING

And Then What Happened?

The Prince married Cinderella. (It pays to have such very small feet.) But soon they started squabbling. 'You married me for my money,' was the Prince's charge. 'You married me for my looks,' was C's reply. 'But your looks will fade, whereas my money will last. Not a fair bargain.' 'No,' said Cinderella and simply walked out.

AND THEN WHAT HAPPENED?

SUNITI NAMJOSHI

Telling tales

Try writing *one* of these:
- a modern version of an old fairy tale
- the sequel to an old fairy tale
- a different ending to an old fairy tale, which will surprise your reader
- a new version of an old fairy tale, retold from an unexpected angle, such as the tale of Little Red Riding Hood told by the big bad wolf, or the tale of Cinderella told by one of the ugly sisters

Extracts

This activity draws attention to:
- [ ] the use of telling detail
- [ ] the importance of setting
- [ ] a sense of plot

Here are three extracts from different novels. Read them carefully and discuss the questions before you start to write.

from: One Day in the Life of Ivan Denisovitch

'Here you are, Alyosha,' said Shukhov, and handed him a biscuit.

Alyosha smiled.

'Thank you. But you've nothing yourself.'

'Eat it.'

(We've nothing but we're always earning.)

Now for that slice of sausage. Into the mouth. Getting your teeth into it. Your teeth. The meaty taste. And the meaty juice, the real stuff. Down it goes, into your belly.

Gone.

The rest, Shukhov decided, for the morning. Before the muster.

And he buried his head in the thin, unwashed blanket, deaf now to the crowd of zeks from the other half as they jostled between the bunk-frames, waiting to be counted.

Shukhov went to sleep fully content. He'd had many strokes of luck that day: they hadn't put him in the cells; they hadn't sent the team to the settlement; he'd pinched a bowl of kasha at dinner; the team-leader had fixed the rates well; he'd built a wall and enjoyed doing it; he'd smuggled that bit of hacksaw-blade through; he'd earned something from Tsezar, in the evening; he'd bought that tobacco. And he hadn't fallen ill. He'd got over it.

A day without a dark cloud. Almost a happy day.

There were three thousand six hundred and fifty-three days like that in his stretch. From the first clang of the rail to the last clang of the rail.

The three extra days were for leap years.

ALEXANDER SOLZHENITSYN

These are the closing lines of a famous short novel.
- What do you think it has been about? For example, can you guess where the men are and how they live?
- What in the passage gave you these impressions? Notice how small details help us to build up a mental picture.

Now write a short chapter for this novel about one of the day's incidents. When you have finished, you may enjoy reading the whole novel.

from: I am the Cheese

I pedal furiously now, not because I want to catch up with them but because this road is deserted and I want to reach a better road or highway as soon as possible. I feel more vulnerable than ever. There are no houses in sight. Most of the cars use the Interstate that runs parallel to this old road. I keep pedalling. There's a curve ahead. Maybe there'll be a house or a new road or something around the curve.

I hear the car again. That unmistakable motor. The car is coming back. The car is rounding the curve, heading in my direction. The car's grille looks like the grinning mouth of some metal monster. The car is pink, a sickly pink, the kind of pink found in vomit. The car thunders by and I see the face of Whipper at the wheel and his grin is as evil and ferocious as the car's grille. The other two guys poke their heads out the window and laugh raucously as they go by.

I reach out and touch my father's package in the basket and I keep pedalling. There is nothing else to do but keep pedalling. I approach the curve and coast for a moment, anticipating rescue there. But there is nothing. Only open fields. Why do the ecologists think we are running out of space on this planet? I've seen so many unoccupied and uninhabited places today that I'm starting to feel lonesome for stores and houses and sidewalks and traffic jams. But now there is a panic in the loneliness. I know the car will come back.

The motor ignites the air again. I hear it coming.

ROBERT CORMIER

This extract comes in the middle of an exciting novel.
- Where do you think it is set?
- What can you tell about the cyclist?
- What do you think has happened earlier?
- What do you think will happen next?

- Where did you get these ideas from?

Now write the rest of the chapter. Afterwards, you could read Robert Cormier's version.

from: *The Secret Garden*

She looked at the key quite a long time. She turned it over and over, and thought about it. As I have said before, she was not a child who had been trained to ask permission or consult her elders about things. All she thought about the key was that if it was the key to the closed garden, and she could find out where the door was, she could perhaps open it and see what was inside the walls, and what had happened to the old rose-trees. It was because it had been shut up so long that she wanted to see it. It seemed as if it must be different from other places and that something strange must have happened to it during ten years. Besides that, if she liked it she could go into it every day and shut the door behind her, and she could make up some play of her own and play it quite alone, because nobody would ever know where she was, but would think the door was still locked and the key buried in the earth. The thought of that pleased her very much.

Living, as it were, all by herself in a house with a hundred mysteriously closed rooms and having nothing whatever to do to amuse herself, had set her inactive brain to work and was actually awakening her imagination. There is no doubt that the fresh, strong, pure air from the moor had a great deal to do with it. Just as it had given her an appetite, and fighting with the wind had stirred her blood, so the same thing had stirred her mind. In India she had always been too hot and languid and weak to care much about anything, but in this place she was beginning to care and to want to do new things. Already she felt less 'contrary', though she did not know why.

She put the key in her pocket and walked up and down her walk. No one but herself ever seemed to come there, so she could walk slowly and look at the wall, or, rather, at the ivy growing on it. The ivy was the baffling thing. Howsoever carefully she looked, she could see nothing but thickly growing, glossy, dark green leaves. She was very much disappointed. Something of her contrariness came back to her as she paced the wall and looked over it at the tree-tops inside. It seemed so silly, she said to herself, to be near it and not be able to get in. She took the key in her pocket when she went back to the house, and she made up her mind that she would always carry it with her when she went out, so that if she ever should find the hidden door she would be ready.

FRANCES HODGSON-BURNETT

- Discuss what you learn about the girl from this passage: her life, her personality and her state of mind.
- Which details in the passage helped you to your conclusions?
- Imagine that she finds the garden door to which the key

Telling tales

belongs. Write the chapter in which she finds, enters and explores the secret garden. Later, you can compare your work with the writer's own version (Chapter 9 of *The Secret Garden*).

Here are two examples written by students after reading the extract:

Her imagination began to run wild. Fear and anticipation washed over her in waves and for a second she wondered if she ought to swing open this old door which had been shut and locked for a reason which was unknown to her. The other fear was greater – the fear of disappointment. A whole week of fantasy could be blown away like dust particles leaving her feeling bare and naked.

Her curiosity won over and with all her strength she turned the old lock and pushed at the door to open. It groaned and creaked as if welcoming life to enter its private world, like a sentry giving permission to go forth.

As she crept apprehensively around the door, the world seemed to stand still. Silence rang in her ears and the bright sunlight made everything shine and glisten with welcome.

Ahead of her was a small winding path made of pebbles large and small, each one alive with sunlight. In between the pebbles were grass and weeds stretching their way up to the warm breeze and bright blinding light.

On either side of this tiny path was long grass waving slightly. The grass reached her waist and was full of flowers, insects and warmth, beckoning her to go down the path.

She moved freely about her garden and explored every inch, noticing the smallest detail, from the cool dark corners smelling of damp earth to the brightly lit centre waving in the breeze.

Every insect, no matter how small, now shared her secret and this pleased her, but what pleased her most of all was that this was her garden, her secret and her key. No-one could take this from her. . . .

KATY PARKS

She parted the fronds and leapt back suddenly as a bird flew out, screeching its annoyance. She cautiously ventured near again, and pulled away some handfuls of ivy. There, in an ivy-less area about a foot square was an area of dark wood. She'd found it, she thought. She tore away at the ivy until at last she'd uncovered the wooden door. There was no keyhole, no handle. Just a sliding bolt set at the top right of the door. She applied a little pressure. Nothing happened. She hit it with the palm of her hand, and the bolt shot back with a sharp grating noise, as rust-flecks sprinkled her face. She pushed the door, and slowly it opened.

She shut her eyes as she entered. She wanted to suddenly be faced with her new world all at once. She leant back against the door and it came to rest against the wooden frame. Slowly she opened her eyes.

The first thing she saw was the statue directly in front of her. It was polished black marble, and was of a woman holding a baby in her arms. She looked to the left. Immaculately kept rosebeds lay alongside neatly clipped lawns with perfectly straight edges. To the right, the same except the flowers were tulips, or so she thought. Each flower stood perfectly straight in weedless, recently-turned earth. Behind the statue was a pond, circular in shape and with another statue on a plinth in the middle. This was a white marble horse, and on it a soldier of the Queen's Army, complete with bushy handlebar moustache and monocle. On his belt was a sword and an old flintlock revolver. He was staring straight ahead, sitting erect in the saddle. The pond was completely clear of any vegetation except for a row of lily pads one pad deep around the perimeter of the pond. She peered over the edge. The pond was about knee-deep and had bright orange fish about a hand's-length long swimming around in it.

This enclosed garden was smaller than she had imagined. She could run to opposite ends in about ten seconds. She walked round to the other side of the pond. Lying down on the stone wall of the pond was a hoe, with fresh earth stuck on the metal blade. Someone had been looking after her garden.

GEOFFREY INNS

5 Journeys in your mind

Journeys, whether real or imaginary, have always stimulated the imagination of writers and readers alike. Not only are they varied and interesting to write about, but they are easy to structure: every journey has a beginning, a middle and an end.

This chapter offers you a number of different journeys to write about, from secret missions to a town trail. It will ask you to write for a variety of purposes and a variety of readers.

Travelogues

This activity tries to encourage:
- [ ] your powers of description
- [ ] your ability to re-create mood
- [ ] the expression of personal impressions and memories

Travelogues are accounts of journeys or expeditions. They can range from the very familiar to the exotic and unusual. They can be real or imaginary. They can be exciting, frightening or amusing, but they are all based on very close observation, and aim to re-create for the reader a real feeling of the place visited. A travelogue is not limited to descriptions of scenery but concentrates on the people and experiences encountered by the traveller.

You might try writing a travelogue about:
- your most recent holiday
- a train journey
- your own journey to school
- an imaginary journey to an exotic place

Your work may take the form of:
- a traveller's notebook or diary, complete with illustrations, postcards and souvenirs.

- a series of letters sent to friends and family back home
- a chapter from a longer travel book

Here are some extracts from travelogues, from the early 1700s to the present day. *Gulliver's Travels* is one of the best-known travel books in the world. Even though the journey was an imaginary one, many people thought it was true when it was first published in 1726!

TRAVELS

INTO SEVERAL

Remote Nations

OF THE

WORLD.

IN FOUR PARTS.

By *LEMUEL GULLIVER*,
firſt a Surgeon, and then a Captain
of ſeveral SHIPS.

VOL. I.

LONDON:
Printed for Benj. Motte, *at the Middle Temple-Gate in* Fleet-ſtreet.
M, DCC, XXVI.

Journeys in your mind

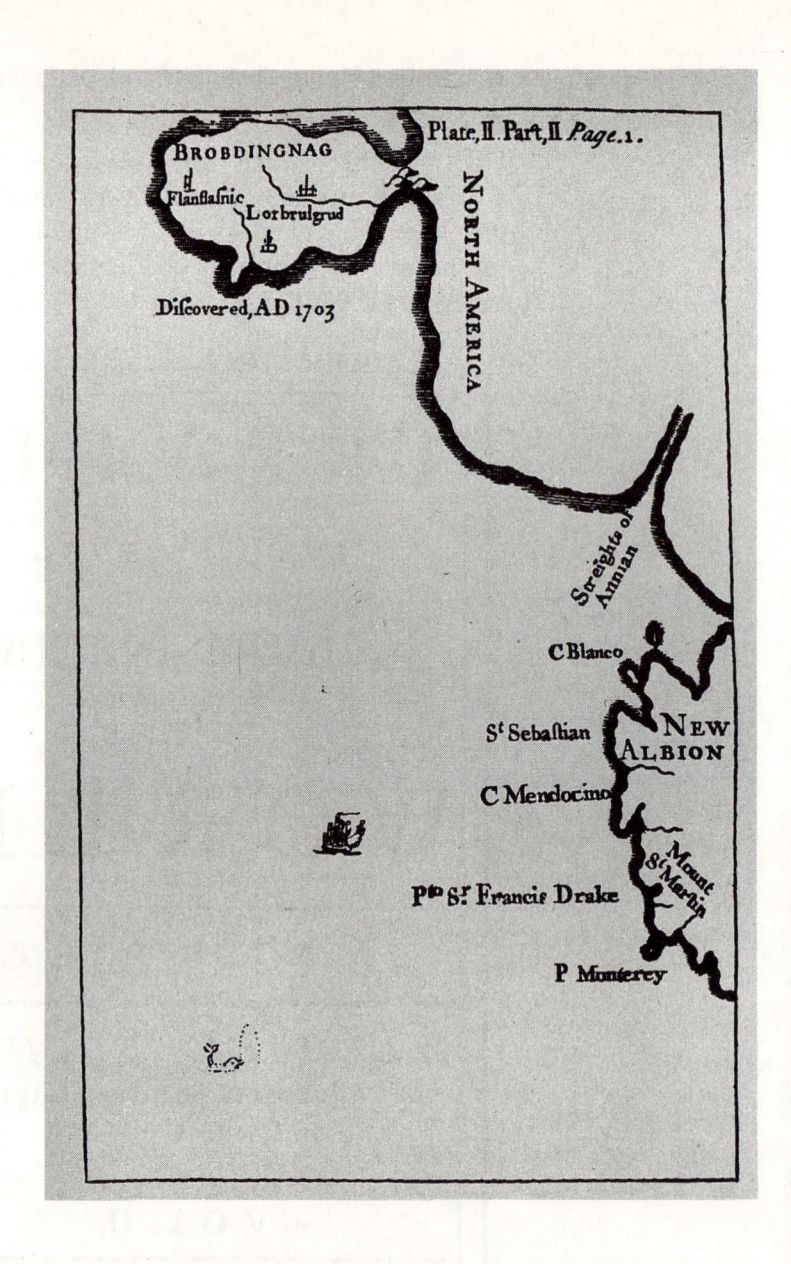

from: Gulliver's Travels

CHAPTER I

A great storm described. The long-boat sent to fetch water, the author goes with it to discover the country. He is left on shore, is seized by one of the natives, and carried to a farmer's house. His reception there, with several accidents that happened there. A description of the inhabitants.

We then set sail, and had a good voyage till we passed the Straits of Madagascar; but having got northward of that island, and to about five degrees south latitude, the winds, which in those seas are observed to blow a constant equal gale between the north and west from the beginning of December to the beginning of May, on the 19th of April began to blow with much greater violence, and more westerly than usual, continuing so for twenty days together, during which time we were driven a little to the east of the Molucca Islands, and about three degrees northward of the Line, as our captain found by an observation he took the 2nd of May, at which time the wind ceased, and it was a perfect calm, whereat I was not a little rejoiced. But he, being a man well experienced in the navigation of those seas, bid us all prepare against a storm, which accordingly happened the day following: for a southern wind, called the southern *monsoon*, began to set in.

JONATHAN SWIFT

from: *A Tour through the Whole Island of Great Britain*

It is easy to conceive how Beverley became a town from this very article, namely, that all the thieves, murtherers, housebreakers and bankrupts, fled hither for protection; and here they obtained safety from the law whatever their crimes night be.

DANIEL DEFOE

from: *Sentimental Journey*

I think there is a fatality in it – I seldom go to the place I set out for.

LAURENCE STERNE

from: **The Letters of Thomas Gray**

Versailles, May 1739

Well! and is this the great front of Versailles? What a huge heap of littleness!

Extracts from an outline for a Book of Travels

Proposals for printing by Subscription, in

THIS LARGE
LETTER

The Travels of T: G: GENT: which will consist of the following Particulars.

CHAP: I.

The Author arrives at Dover; his conversation with the Mayor of that Corporation; sets out in the Pacquet-Boat, grows very sick; the Author spews, a very minute account of all the circumstances thereof: his arrival at Calais; how the inhabitants of that country speak French, & are said to be all Papishes; the Author's reflexions thereupon.

2.

How they feed him with Soupe, & what Soupe is. how he meets with a Capucin; & what a Capucin is. how they shut him up in a Post-Chaise, & send him to Paris; he goes wondring along dureing 6 days; & how there are Trees, & Houses just as in England. arrives at Paris without knowing it.

4.

Goes to the Opera; grand Orchestra of Humstrums, Bagpipes, Salt-boxes, Tabours, & Pipes. Anatomy on a French Ear, shewing the formation of it to be entirely different from that of an English one, & that Sounds have a directly contrary effect upon one & the other....

5.

The Author takes unto him a Taylour. his Character. how he covers him with Silk, & Fringe, & widens his figure with buckram a yard on each side; Wastcoat, & Breeches so strait, he can neither breath, nor walk. how the Barber curls him en Bequille, & à la negligee, & ties a vast Solitaire about his Neck; how the Milliner lengthens his ruffles to his finger's ends, & sticks his two arms into a Muff. how he cannot stir, & how they cut him in proportion to his Clothes.

7.

Goes into the Country to Rheims in Champagne. stays there 3 Months, what he did there (he must beg the reader's pardon, but) he has really forgot.

8.

Proceeds to Lyons. Vastness of that City. Can't see the Streets for houses. how rich it is, & how much it stinks. Poem upon the Confluence of the Rhône, & the Saône, by a friend of the Author's; very pretty!

9.

Makes a journey into Savoy, & in his way visits the Grande Chartreuse; he is set astride upon a Mule's back, & begins to climb up the Mountain. Rocks & Torrents beneath; Pine-trees, & Snows above; horrours, & terrours on all sides. the Author dies of the Fright.

THOMAS GRAY

from: *Journey Through Britain*

A boxer's remedy for a walker's pains

In a Bristol hotel the next morning I thought the walk had come to an end. Overworked calf muscles seemed to have gone on strike. They had seized up. Despite hot baths and amateurish attempts at massage, I could scarcely walk for more than a few paces without wincing.

A long distance telephone call to an old friend in the medical business confirmed what I knew: that I needed rest; that I should take things easy. I would be advised, he said, to get some professional attention, locally. It could be serious. I shouldn't fool around with myself. And so on.

JOHN HILLABY

from: The Great Railway Bazaar

Then, past a row of semi-detached houses, we entered a tunnel, and after travelling a minute in complete darkness we were shot wonderfully into a new setting, open meadows, cows cropping grass, farmers haying in blue jackets. We had surfaced from London, a grey sodden city that lay underground. At Sevenoaks there was another tunnel, another glimpse of the pastoral, fields of pawing horses, some kneeling sheep, crows on an oasthouse, and a swift sight of a settlement of prefab houses out one window. Out the other window, a Jacobean farmhouse and more cows. That is England: the suburbs overlap the farms. At several level crossings the country lanes were choked with cars, backed up for a hundred yards.

PAUL THEROUX

from: Journeys

I arrived at the scene of the accident shortly after the event, and the country road was still half-blocked by the muddle of it. The truck was overturned in the ditch; both the bullock carts were toppled broken on their sides, their big wooden wheels ungainly in the air, their ripped sacks spilling grain across the highway. Three men whom I took to be the drivers were sitting motionless on their haunches at the edge of the road, and under the trees a little huddle of women was talking in a high-pitched but muted gabble, very fast, nervously. An old man in a dhoti walked round and round the wreckage, prodding it with his stick and coughing.

Rivulets of glutinous dark blood ran away down the camber of the road to the gutter, collecting down there in a puddle, a few leaves already floating in it from the trees above. One of the bullocks had been torn open right along its flank, and guts were oozing obscenely from its smooth skin. The other animal was bleeding heavily through the nostrils, and even as I watched it raised its head a little, with a sort of gurgle at the mouth, and then dropped it heavily on to the ground again. The old man prodded it inquisitively with his stick. The three squatters did not stir. 'Drive on,' I said.

JAN MORRIS

Mission Improbable

In this activity you will have to:
- ☐ present information clearly
- ☐ issue clear instructions
- ☐ keep an accurate record of your actions.

Work in groups.

You are The Leader, shadowy head of the secret Mission Improbable team, a small group of experts who tackle only the most dangerous and difficult rescue missions. In order to maintain maximum security you yourself never meet the team: instead you send them a folder of information and a tape explaining the mission....

There is trouble on the distant island of Zark. An aircraft carrying a famous professor has been forced by an unknown power to land. Before the last radio transmission came to an abrupt end, you learnt that the professor was being held by armed personnel, and that he or she was carrying files of TOP SECRET information.

Provide the Mission Improbable team with all the details they will need to mount a rescue mission as safely and as speedily as possible. (Of course, if you know of another

Journeys in your mind

mission more urgent than the one on Zark you should provide details of that instead.) You could include:
- A detailed map of Zark, based on reconnaissance information.

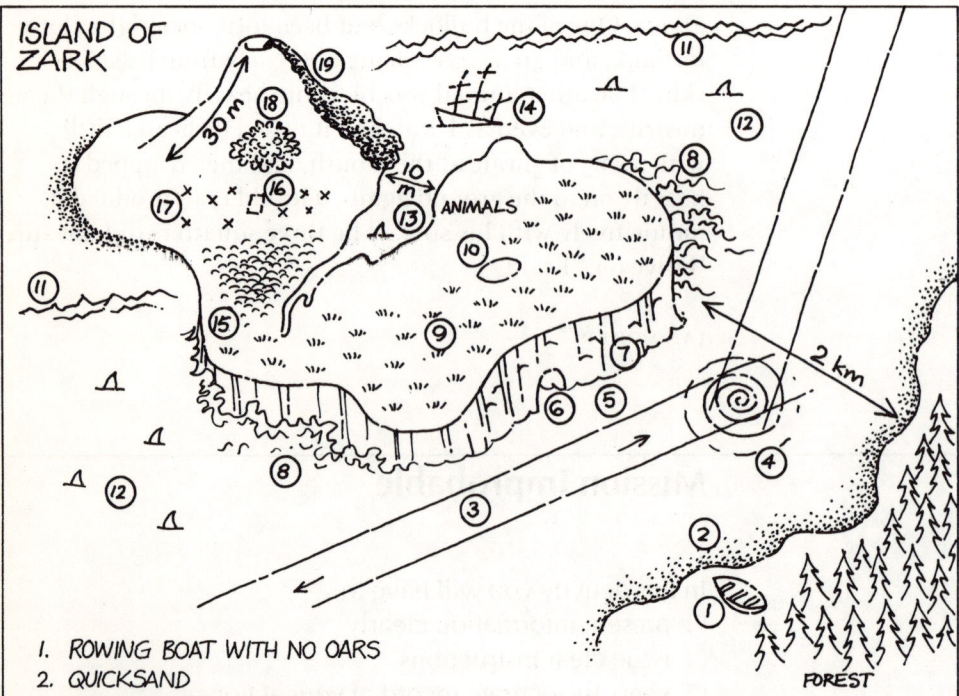

ISLAND OF ZARK

1. ROWING BOAT WITH NO OARS
2. QUICKSAND
3. STRONG CROSS CURRENTS
4. WHIRLPOOL
5. CALM WATER
6. ENTRANCE TO TUNNEL SYSTEM
7. STEEP CLIFFS WITH LEDGES WHERE THERE ARE NESTING GULLS
8. SHEER CLIFFS AND WHITE WATER
9. MARSHLAND
10. EXIT FROM THE TUNNEL
11. REEF
12. SHARKS
13. SHARKS MOVE INTO THIS INLET AT NIGHT
14. SHIPWRECK BLOCKS THE ENTRANCE TO THE INLET
15. MUD WHICH GIVES OFF A POISONOUS GAS
16. SECRET DOOR WHICH ONLY SHOWS UP IN THE MOONLIGHT
17. BOOBY TRAPS
18. DEADLY PLANTS COVERING THE ENTRANCE TO A MAZE OF TUNNELS WHICH LEAD TO THE CENTRE OF THE VOLCANO
19. MOLTEN LAVA

Outline map of Zark

- A suggested outline plan (leaving details to the team).
- Pen-portraits and relevant information about the suspected kidnappers.
- A list of equipment and resources – remember that the team travel light.
- A tape-recording to explain the situation, with any additional information you may receive during planning.

Place all this information in a folder marked TOP SECRET and pass it to another group in your class. The team are to write in their log book a report on how the mission goes. You can do the same for *their* mission.

Mounting an expedition

In this activity, you will need to present a case:
☐ persuasively
☐ with clarity and logic
☐ to demonstrate thoroughness and efficiency

Henry J. Timpson III is a multi-millionaire who believes in helping young people to become self-reliant and productive members of society. To this end he will provide funds to mount expeditions to unexplored parts of the world or for a particularly valuable purpose.

You have to submit a proposal for funds, explaining in detail where you want to go and what you want to do. Unfortunately, the number of awards is limited, so you are in competition with any other applicants (groups and individuals).

To help you in formulating your application, here is Henry Timpson's personal checklist which he uses to shortlist the best applications:
- ☐ worthwhile purpose?
- ☐ obvious enthusiasm?
- ☐ realistic planning?
- ☐ previous experience? (any records or cuttings?)
- ☐ safety and survival plans?
- ☐ thorough research?
- ☐ evidence of efficiency, thoughtfulness, good organisation?

Imaginary island

This activity should help you:
- ☐ to exercise your imagination
- ☐ to write for a wider audience
- ☐ to use a variety of styles

Imagine an island.
- Draw its outline.
- Imagine its landscape, climate, people and history – these may be very unusual.
- Think up a name.
- Fill in your map.

You are the island's first visitor and you stay for one week.
- Keep a *journal* to record each day's experiences, discoveries and adventures.
- Gather together a *catalogue* of the island's unusual plants and animals.
- Make a *scroll* containing all the laws of the island, along with a brief account of its system of justice.

- Prepare an island *guide* for future visitors, pointing out interesting and beautiful features.
- Record an *interview* with an interesting inhabitant.
- Write a brief *history* of the island.
- Write an *article* for a magazine back home about any feature of island life which you find fascinating.

Town trail

This activity asks you:
☐ to write informatively
☐ to give simple, clear directions
☐ to interest the general reader

Many towns now publish 'town trails' to guide visitors around local beauty spots and to point out historical features.

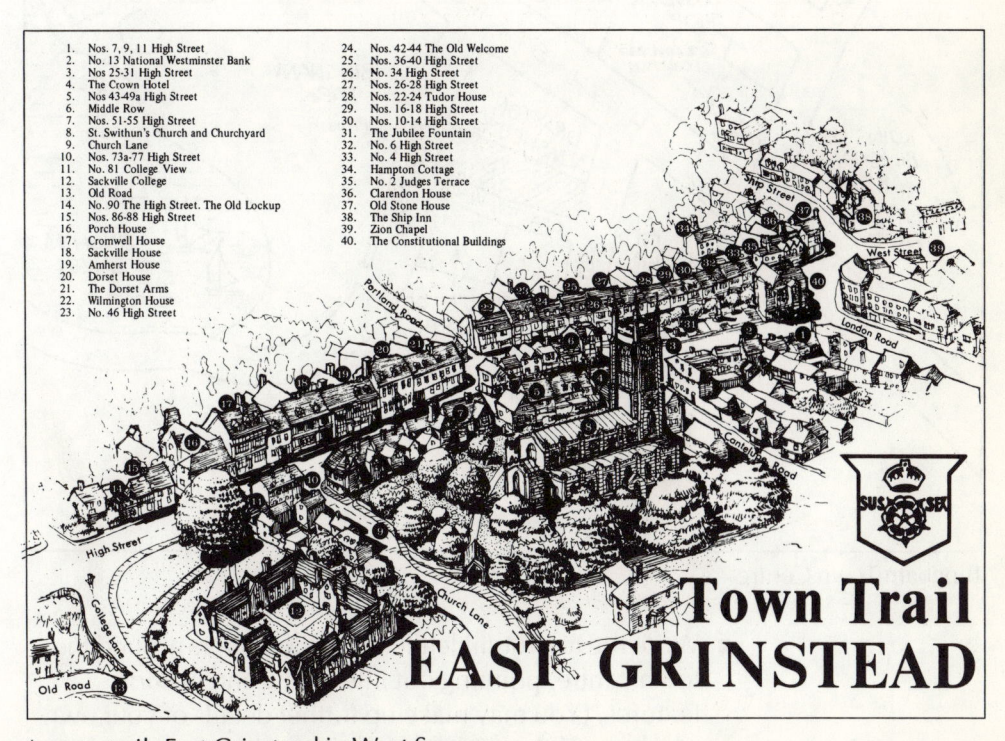

1. Nos. 7, 9, 11 High Street
2. No. 13 National Westminster Bank
3. Nos 25-31 High Street
4. The Crown Hotel
5. Nos 43-49a High Street
6. Middle Row
7. Nos. 51-55 High Street
8. St. Swithun's Church and Churchyard
9. Church Lane
10. Nos. 73a-77 High Street
11. No. 81 College View
12. Sackville College
13. Old Road
14. No. 90 The High Street. The Old Lockup
15. Nos. 86-88 High Street
16. Porch House
17. Cromwell House
18. Sackville House
19. Amherst House
20. Dorset House
21. The Dorset Arms
22. Wilmington House
23. No. 46 High Street
24. Nos. 42-44 The Old Welcome
25. Nos. 36-40 High Street
26. No. 34 High Street
27. Nos. 26-28 High Street
28. Nos. 22-24 Tudor House
29. Nos. 16-18 High Street
30. Nos. 10-14 High Street
31. The Jubilee Fountain
32. No. 6 High Street
33. No. 4 High Street
34. Hampton Cottage
35. No. 2 Judges Terrace
36. Clarendon House
37. Old Stone House
38. The Ship Inn
39. Zion Chapel
40. The Constitutional Buildings

A town trail: East Grinstead in West Sussex

Journeys in your mind

Bingham is a beautiful but little-known town which has several attractions that might interest visitors. Bingham Town Council has decided to publish a town-trail leaflet for visitors, entitled *See Bingham in One Hour*.

- Look carefully at the map and information provided. Work out a simple tour of the town centre for visitors on foot.

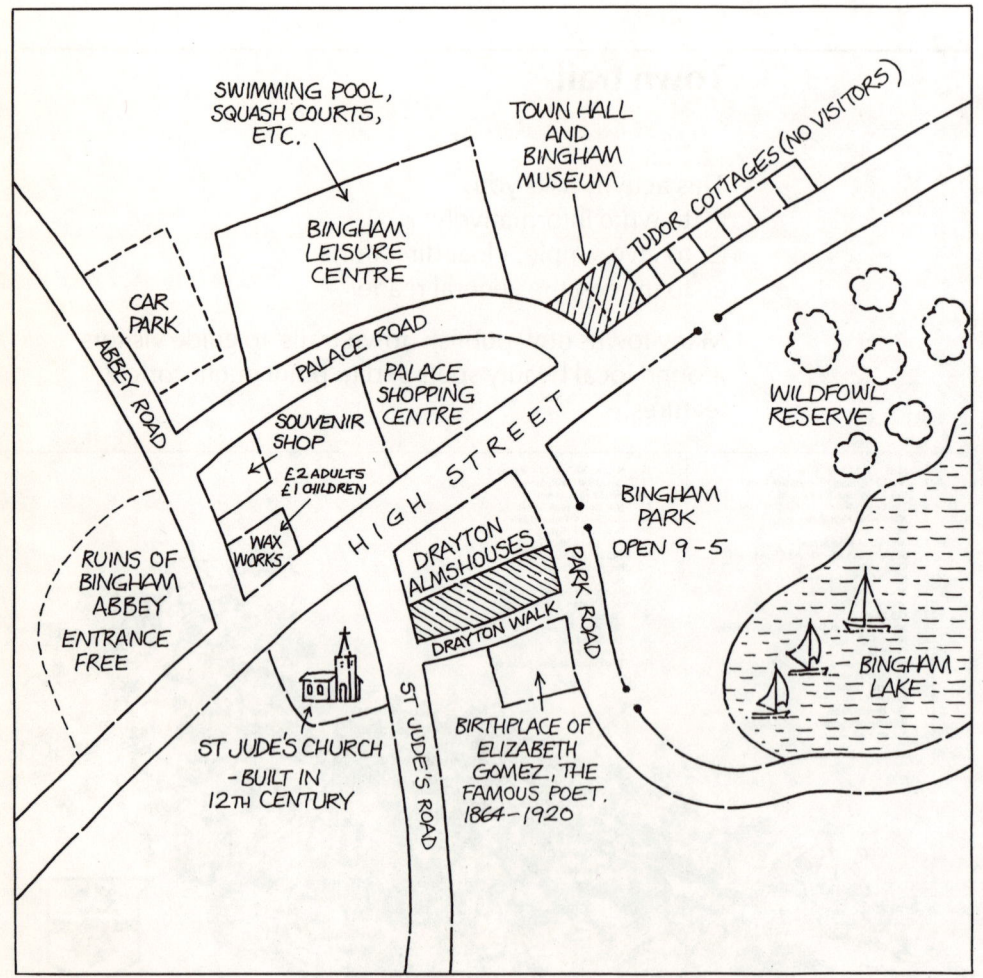

Bingham Town Centre

- Write the town-trail leaflet to guide visitors around the town centre, pointing out interesting and historic features. (You may make up further details of your own and include these in the leaflet.)

6 Publications

A great deal of what we read has been published by companies which employ writers, printers, sales representatives and so on. Besides school books like this one, what other publications can you think of? There are novels, magazines, newspapers ... what else? Make a list.

All of these publications are produced by publishers who choose what to publish, and who try to find out what sorts of people might buy them. Look around the books in your classroom. Can you find the names of publishers on them?

In this chapter we want *you* to become a publisher and to consider what is involved in the creation of public writing. You will need to consider:
- what you want written
- how to organise the talents and written work of other people
- how to select the best pieces
- how to present the chosen material
- how to attract readers

Book covers

In this exercise, you are asked to write in a way that is:
- brief but to the point
- informative without giving too much away
- tempting for the reader

Collect a few books with information on the outside covers. Look carefully at what publishers put on the front and back covers of their books.

- Jot down the different *types* of information. Why is the information there, and who is it for?
- Which of the books in front of you do you most fancy

Publications

reading and why? Which of the features on the covers tempted you?

Design and write:
- a book cover for a collection of your own or a friend's stories, which would encourage classmates to read them
- an alternative book cover for a book you have recently read

You may include on your cover some of the readers' comments.

General Editor: Aidan Chambers

Taking Care of CARRUTHERS

One cold, wet
Eugene are en
Carruthers Bea
a sore throat.
cheer him up.
 So Emily T
about the un
friends. Befor
happy he has

M books

Taking Care of CARRUTHERS

DRAMA ANTHOLOGIES

JUNIOR DRAMA WORKSHOP

MACMILLAN

ALAN LAMBERT
BRIAN SCOTT-HUGHES

DRAMA ANTHOLOGIES

MACMILLAN

Macmillan Drama Anthologies offer a series of lively and stimulating play scripts to be read in class or presented for performance. The series is aimed at a range of age-groups, from middle-school to upper-secondary level, and will include scripts in a variety of genres – documentaries, musicals, and radio and TV adaptations. The plays are accompanied by source material and advice on presentation. Follow-up ideas for improvisation, written work and discussion are included so that work on the scripts can be extended in the English or drama lesson.

Junior Drama Workshop

The plays in this volume were first broadcast in the BBC School Radio series *Junior Drama Workshop*. They have been adapted for reading and performing by upper-primary and lower-secondary age pupils.

■ *The Plague Village*   ALAN LAMBERT
The history of the village of Eyam

■ *On the Oregon Trail*   ALAN LAMBERT
One family's experience of the American frontier

■ *Return to the City*   BRIAN SCOTT-HUGHES
What it meant to be an evacuee

Cover picture: BBC Hulton Picture Library

ISBN 0-333-43459-5

MACMILLAN EDUCATION

9 780333 434598

Class magazine

In this exercise, you have to pay special attention to:
- ☐ the interests of your readership
- ☐ creating an attractive and useful lay-out
- ☐ writing in a clear and interesting way

Collect together a wide range of magazines. There are magazines for every age group and all sorts of interests.

- Who do the publishers hope will buy each magazine? How do you know this?
- Look more closely at the range of articles in the magazine. Do you see any similarities from magazine to magazine?
- Now look at the way the contents are laid out. Space in a magazine is valuable and scarce, so the contents have to be arranged carefully and attractively.

Make up your own class magazine.
- Decide who you want to read it, and aim your articles and your style of writing to suit these readers. For example, you might produce:
  - ☐ a magazine for younger pupils
  - ☐ a magazine for another class
  - ☐ a magazine for parents
  - ☐ a magazine for other pupils with a particular interest (e.g. sport, fashion, fishing)
- In a group, compile a list of ideas and articles to include in the magazine, and organise who will do what.

Which Bike?

OCTOBER 50p

EVERY MONTH ALL NEW AND USED BIKE PRICES

FUTURE SHOCK FROM BMW

HONDA AND SUZUKI 550'S TESTED

EXCLUSIVE! HONDA COMPARED WITH

THE NORTON THAT NEVER

ISSUE SEVEN · APRIL 1987 · £1.25

THE ARTIST'S AND ILLUSTRATOR'S MAGAZINE

BUYERS GUIDE
WATERCOLOUR
Picking pans and tubes

OILS
EFFECTS OF LIGHT
A Mediterranean scene

GREAT PAINTERS
J.M.W. TURNER

DRAWING
DRAWING ON LIFE
The Work of Josef Herman

PORTRAIT
QUENTIN BLAKE
A picture book life

VOUCHERS WORTH **£65** FREE INSIDE

Two Great Names Come Together

NT Nursing Mirror
NURSING TIMES

February 25 — March 3, 1987
50p

EVERY NURSE'S NIGHTMARE

Struck off the register: could it happen to you?

PLUS:
- Breast cancer: is information the key?
- What is brain death?
- Computers in nursing
- Sister Plume

NT: MORE JOBS
MORE READERS
MORE FEATURES

Publications

Poetry anthology

This activity will give you experience in:
- [ ] selecting and assessing work for publication
- [ ] writing a critical commentary
- [ ] providing appropriate and attractive illustrations

Your school will probably have several sets of poetry *anthologies* – collections of poems by a number of poets, sometimes accompanied by photographs and illustrations. Opposite is Sue's illustration of William Blake's poem, *The Tyger*.

- Collect together some different anthologies and note down any differences in the way they are presented. You might like to start with these questions:
  - [ ] Are there pictures?
  - [ ] Are the poems grouped in a particular way?
  - [ ] How effective are the covers of the books?
  - [ ] Does the anthology reveal anything about the poems or the poets or the authors?
  - [ ] Is there an introduction? If so, what kind of comments does it make?
- Produce your own anthology of poetry for use with your class or even with another group in school. Collect poems you think will appeal to your chosen readers, and present them as attractively as possible.
- Find photographs, pictures or drawings to suit the poems you have chosen. You can find good material in colour-supplement magazines, or you might like to draw pictures or take photographs yourself.
- Write an introduction to your anthology, and maybe include some details about the poets you have chosen. You could also write a little about each poem, saying why you have chosen it or why you like it.

You could make up an anthology from the work of well-known, established poets or from the poems written by your classmates. You might like to base the anthology on a theme.

THE TYGER

Tyger! Tyger! burning bright
In the forests of the night,
What immortal hand or eye
Could frame thy fearful symmetry?

In what distant deeps or skies
Burnt the fire of thine eyes?
On what wings dare he aspire?
What the hand dare seize the fire?

And what shoulder, & what art,
Could twist the sinews of thy heart?
And when thy heart began to beat,
What dread hand? & what dread feet?

What the hammer? what the chain?
In what furnace was thy brain?
What the anvil? what dread grasp
Dare its deadly terrors clasp?

When the stars threw down their spears
And water'd heaven with their tears,
Did he smile his work to see?
Did he who made the Lamb make thee?

Tyger! Tyger! burning bright
In the forests of the night,
What immortal hand or eye
Dare frame thy fearful symmetry?

William Blake

Commissioning a novel

This activity emphasises the importance of:
- ☐ intriguing openings
- ☐ effective endings
- ☐ an interesting narrative style

Imagine you work for a publishing company. It is your job to spot writing talent.

Your boss wants you to find some promising new novelists. To do this, you must ask other people in your class to submit work on a novel for your consideration. Ask them to write:
- the two opening paragraphs
- the two closing paragraphs
- two paragraphs from the middle of the story

You might want to specify what sort of novel you want, or the title.

If your class is large enough you could split into publishing groups, each one commissioning novel extracts from the others. One group might choose to seek detective novels, another one might prefer romantic novels, and so on.

When you have collected in the work and discussed the merits of each set of extracts, return the work to the writers with your comments, explaining what you have enjoyed in their work and giving tips on how to improve it.

Finally, publish selected pieces either in a folder or as a wall display.

Acknowledgements

The authors and publishers wish to thank the following who have kindly given permission for the use of copyright material:

The *Daily Telegraph* for 'Upside down in a fire drill' by Andrew Watts, 'The postcard' by Guy Carter, 'The inner man' by Christine M. Banks, 'The death touch' by Dawn Hunt and 'A trip to the big wet one' by Matthew Ember, from *The Book of Mini-Sagas*, 1985; Florence Grossman for 'And' by Debi Brenin and 'Snow White's Prince' by Billy Fischling, from *Getting From Here to There* by Florence Grossman, Boynton/Cook Inc.; Daniel Keyes for an extract from *Flowers for Algernon*, Robert P. Mills, New York. Copyright © 1959, 1987 by Daniel Keyes; Penguin Books Ltd. for an extract from *The Diary of a Farmer's Wife 1796–1797* by Anne Hughes, Allen Lane, 1980. Copyright © Mollie Preston 1937, 1964, 1980; Sheba Feminist Publishers for *Bird Woman, The Doll* and *And Then What Happened* by Suniti Namjoshi.

The authors and publishers wish to acknowledge the following photograph sources:

Reproduced with the permission of British Telecom, p. 65; The East Grinstead Society/Mr D G Joyce, p. 101; Penguin Books Ltd, illustrations from Gulliver's Travels by Jonathan Swift, p. 91/92; Transworld Publishers Ltd, from Making Magic © 1976 by Malcolm Carrick, p. 64.

The authors and publishers would also like to thank the Thomas Bennett Community College for permission to use the 'Super Speller' cartoon, and Sue Breach for the illustration of *The Tyger*.

Every effort has been made to trace all the copyright holders, but if any have been inadvertently overlooked the publishers will be pleased to make the necessary arrangements at the first opportunity.

Illustrations by Illustra Design Ltd and Taurus Graphics.

Our thanks also to the people who hand wrote the various letters and articles included in this book.